PENGUIN BOOKS

De-Junk Your Mind

De-Junk Your Mind

Simple Solutions for Positive Living

Dawna Walter

PENGUIN BOOKS

PENGUIN BOOKS

Published by the Penguin Group
Penguin Books Ltd, 80 Strand, London WC2R 0RL, England
Penguin Books (USA) Inc., 375 Hudson Street, New York, New York 10014, USA
Penguin Group (Canada), 10 Alcorn Avenue, Toronto, Ontario, Canada M4V 3B2
(a division of Pearson Penguin Canada Inc.)
Penguin Ireland, 25 St Stephen's Green, Dublin 2, Ireland
(a division of Penguin Books Ltd)
Penguin Group (Australia), 250 Camberwell Road,
Camberwell, Victoria 3124, Australia (a division of Pearson Australia Group Pty Ltd)
Penguin Books India Pvt Ltd, 11 Community Centre,
Panchsheel Park, New Delhi – 110 017, India
Penguin Group (NZ), cnr Airborne and Rosedale Roads, Albany,
Auckland 1310, New Zealand (a division of Pearson New Zealand Ltd)
Penguin Books (South Africa) (Pty) Ltd, 24 Sturdee Avenue,
Rosebank 2196, South Africa

Penguin Books Ltd, Registered Offices: 80 Strand, London WC2R 0RL, England

www.penguin.com

First published 2005
1

Set in 11.75/14.75 pt Monotype Minion
Typeset by Rowland Phototypesetting Ltd, Bury St Edmunds, Suffolk
Printed in England by Clays Ltd, St Ives plc

For my mother, 'the Gooch', who at 94 proves the theory that you are only as old as you think you are.

Keep on rocking.

Contents

Introduction: De-Junk Your Mind

I have a really simple view of life. We're here for a good time, not a long time, so make every minute count. By making each minute count, it doesn't mean that you have to achieve something each waking moment. And it doesn't mean that you have to continuously work yourself to death towards some magic time in your life when you feel that you are finally able to take a break or do the things you really want to do. What it does mean is that you find things in every moment that delight you and make you feel good. The only thing that prevents you from doing this is the mental baggage you carry around with you, which prevents you from seeing things clearly due to old patterns and beliefs. So where does the mental baggage come from? Like the physical clutter in your home, mental clutter slowly creeps up over the years without your even noticing. It starts with attitudes and beliefs that you learn as a child that shape how you view yourself in the world. It is compounded by habits that develop over time whereby you take your eye off the ball and go through the motions rather than truly experience the moment. And it is made worse still by the self-destructive cycle of carrying around the negative experiences that have happened in your life and using them as a basis to judge future experiences. Everyone has mental baggage, but it doesn't have to stop you dead in your tracks.

We live in a society where we turn on the news and see death and destruction and read papers that warn us of global catastrophes. Not only do we worry about current events in the world, we worry about the events that happened during our parents' lifetime and their parents' lifetime. We worry about the food we eat, the people that are around us, and all these things weigh you down and prevent you from finding new and exciting ways to live your life to the fullest.

There are so many social norms that we feel we have to live up to, and each expectation that we feel the need to meet, rather than the desire to have, will feel like a burden. If you are expected to be a doctor because everyone in your family is a doctor, it's fantastic if that is what you really want to be. But if you choose to be a doctor in order not to disappoint those around you, you will never express your true personality and may never feel happy and satisfied in what you do. The same is true for sexual preference, marriage, children, career choice and any decision that you make based on other people's expectations. How many times do you make choices that don't feel right in order to get approval and fit in? If you make them, how often do you think, 'What if I had chosen differently?'

We judge ourselves by other people's success and feel bad when we haven't lived up to someone else's dreams. We worry if a colleague gets a pay rise, if our house isn't as nice as someone else's or when friends get married and have babies and we are still single and childless. Rather than focusing on what you don't have, which always makes you feel bad, you can learn to harness your energy to get the things you truly do want out of life by clearing your mind of negative energy patterns.

It always feels better to dream about the things you want rather than think about the things you don't have. It is absolutely astonishing what you are able to see when you look for it. If I told you to go outside and find a spot in nature that you think is beautiful, you wouldn't think twice, because you know what beauty is and can see it and find it when you want to. And even if I told you to think about your favourite spot in the world and create it in your mind, you could do that as well, because when you enjoy an experience, it feels good and it lasts a lifetime. How often do you look at the beauty that surrounds you each day? How often do you think about all the wonderful experiences that you have had and all the people who love and care about you?

However, if I told you to look in the mirror and list your most beautiful features, could you do the same? If I asked you to make a list of the twenty things you do best, would you find it easy to do? If I asked you to write down 50 reasons why you are loveable, how would you rate? Do you look for the best you have to offer or do you look at the things you think of as faults? What do you think feels better?

You know what, we all have stuff! Each and every one of us has had experiences that we would not choose to have again. We have experienced loss and disappointment and physical injuries or aches and pains. We succeed at some things and are not so good at others. We have all done things that we wish we hadn't, said things in the moment without thinking, and that is what makes us human. All these things happened in a moment in time that you cannot revisit. What you can do is look at what you learned from the experience and choose differently next time you are faced with a similar situation.

De-junking your mind is easier than you think. It doesn't take years of therapy to try to understand what has happened in the past, for how can you ever understand other people's motives, or events that happen that are out of your control? All it takes is to re-examine some of your ways of thinking that junk up your mind and keep you reliving the same unpleasant experiences over and over again. By forgiving yourself and others for all that has happened in the past, you free up space in your mind to allow in new things. Once you look at each minute and see what that minute has to offer, you will never look back.

Starting at this very moment, you can choose to focus on a thought that uplifts you rather than drags you down. You can take action to get the things you want right now in the moment, and when you string all of these moments together you will find that you feel good, accomplish more and have a lot more fun in the process. It always feels better to take a small step forward than to worry about achieving the bigger goals that can easily overwhelm you.

Over the last 10 years I have helped many people de-junk their physical possessions from their homes and offices in order to alleviate the confusion and chaos that arise from having too many things around you. Although sometimes the situation arises from a lack of time or not having organizational skills, hoarding is more often a symptom of underlying emotional issues. Once you become aware of your reasons for holding on to things, it is much easier to break the cycle and release the old patterns of behaviour.

Like physical clutter, mental clutter also causes confusion and chaos and prevents you from fully enjoying your life. Just by spending a bit of time thinking about some of your attitudes, beliefs and habits, you can easily identify the ones that no longer work for you.

This book is intended to help you to de-junk your mind of things that are holding you back and to get you on a positive track towards gaining more enjoyment out of everything you do each day.

The first section of the book helps you to look at some of the influences in your life which make you the person you are today. You will find that some things you have learned or experienced are no longer relevant to your life, but still impact on how you feel about yourself, your relationships and professional life. There are many simple exercises throughout the book to help you let go of these unwanted feelings and gain confidence in the process.

I am a firm believer in the power of positive thinking as the easiest way to have a happy and fulfilled life. Once you shed the negative thought cycle and habits, there are many ways in which to develop a positive mental attitude. I sincerely believe that you can do anything you want to do, if you set your mind to it, and by putting into practice some simple strategies that I have used for many years, you can immediately start to gain the benefits of a positive attitude in everything you do. With a positive attitude it is easier to achieve your bigger life goals.

There are some key life skills that I have found most useful in helping me to accomplish my goals. Learning to speak up and effectively communicate with those around you helps you to release things that may be cluttering up your mind. It also gives you a much greater chance of successfully getting what you want. There are many techniques in this book to help you sharpen your communication skills in both your personal and professional life.

I have also found that many people have a difficult time keeping things in perspective. Looking for solutions, rather than focusing on the negative aspects of the problem, can easily solve what seems like an enormous problem in the moment. Keeping things in perspective helps to lessen the stress and strain of unexpected events that occur in all of our lives. It also helps you to prioritize what is most important for you on a daily basis.

Life need not be complicated. There are so many ways that

you can easily improve the quality of your life that only require one thing – your desire to do them. At the end of the book I have included a list of my favourite ways to instantly feel better that always work for me, and I hope you try them out and see how you feel. I am confident that they will work for you.

I know that, like having a good spring clean at home, once you begin to shed the mental clutter you will feel lighter, more energetic and ready to face each new day for all that it has to offer. I hope that you are able to feel the healing energy in these words I write and that they enable you to see things in a different light.

Life is beautiful.

Dawna Walter

1.
Who Are You?

The first step towards getting rid of a big chunk of mental clutter is to free yourself of old attitudes and beliefs that are outdated. Let me start by saying that I am not heavily into endless self-analysis. I know many people who go from one therapy to another trying to figure out why the things that have happened to them in their lives have happened. They keep delving back to past unpleasant experiences and reliving them over and over again. It didn't feel very good the first time around and it doesn't get any better when you live it over again. Why make yourself feel miserable?

My approach is to not look at why, as often there is no way of answering this question. Who can say why some people are born into terribly difficult circumstances and others into lives of great privilege? Who can answer for other people's actions? Who can explain death, war and other events in the world? Rather than looking at why the situation has happened, an easier and more productive approach is to look at how you reacted or handled the situation.

Just by taking a few minutes to write down the first things that come to mind when answering the questions throughout this chapter, you will gain a lot of insight into your beliefs, attitudes and some areas in your life that could benefit from a re-think. Once you are able to define an area that needs de-junking, further chapters will enable you to break old habits, routines and attitudes to help you better focus on getting more of what you want each day.

In order to control your reactions, it is important to explore the behaviour patterns that keep you making choices that don't make you feel good. Sometimes these choices are based simply on habit. You do the same thing over and over again because at some point in time you learned to do it. You may have learned it from a figure of authority and were not in a position to question whether you liked it or not, and continued the practice because it was expected of you. A good example of this is eating habits. If as a child you were forced to eat everything on your plate, your attitude towards food could be that you always have to eat everything on your plate – whether you like it or not and even whether it feels good or not. It is easy to see how the things you learn in childhood can affect your attitudes today. We will further explore your habits in the next chapter.

The greatest thing about reaching the age of maturity is that you have unlimited personal choice. You can question what feels right or wrong for you, and make choices based on what makes you, as an individual, feel good. Feeling good is your natural and harmonious state of being and when you feel good, what you are doing and thinking are the right choices to help you attain your desires. Any areas of your life that don't make you feel good in yourself are the areas where you find yourself in situations you don't want to be in. If you don't make the choice to get what you want, who will?

I sincerely believe that we all have the innate ability to know what feels good and what doesn't. If I asked you to sit down and make a list of 50 things that make you feel good, I would like to think that you could easily do it and add another 50! Just as you learned that something hot will burn you so you don't deliberately touch something hot, re-programming your habits and changing your attitudes will enable you to stay away from the situations and experiences that have not felt good in the past. Often, the only thing that gets in the way of making those choices is the fear of the unknown. You have always done something in the same way and, therefore, you are hesitant to try something new – even if the old way doesn't work for you. My question to you is, what is the harm in trying?

There is no one else exactly like you

There are many factors that make you the individual that you are today. Some things, such as your physical characteristics, are genetic – a combination of both your parents and their families' traits and features which will differ between you and your siblings, unless you are an identical twin.

Other factors, such as your education, cultural background and spirituality shape how you have viewed the world up to this moment. Looking back at the things you have learned helps you to reconnect with some of your fundamental beliefs and can also help you to discard things you have been taught but proven to be out of line with your current way of thinking. A bit of quiet introspection is a great way to come to grips with your current likes and dislikes, to enable you to make the necessary changes towards leading a more fulfilling life.

Although these beliefs and values may shape how you view the world to this present time, many people adopt their own values and beliefs as they continue to experience new things. If everyone thought the same way, there would never be any new inventions and the ramifications of that are awesome.

There are many other factors that can impact on how you view the world. The people you come into contact with throughout your life have influenced your decisions and thoughts and even how you feel about yourself. You can probably think back to a teacher, friend or loved one who told you how good you were at something. This little bit of encouragement gave you the confidence to believe in yourself and to pursue your interest. Likewise, if you had the experience of someone telling you that you were bad at something, you would probably come to believe that as well. At a young age you could not choose the people that you came in contact with. But now you can. We will explore how the people you have in your life have influenced your course of action.

Writing your thoughts down is a great way to get things out of your system. Often, things can come to mind that you never thought of before and it helps you to get a clearer understanding of where you are. Even if you never read it again, seeing things in black and white is a great way to get your attention.

Always start in a positive and relaxed frame of mind. Sitting in a comfortable chair with your feet on the ground and your back firmly supported, close your eyes and take in a good deep breath to the count of four, then exhale to the count of four, making sure to keep your shoulders in a downward and relaxed position. Do this a few times and then slowly open your eyes and think about one question at a time. Write down whatever comes to mind without judging the answers.

What we learned from our parents

For most of us, our parents are probably the greatest influence in our life. Most of you will have grown up with one or both of your biological parents who, first and foremost, created you. Whether your birth was planned or not, your parents chose to bring you into this world. This is one of the most serious decisions that can be made in a lifetime and for most people it is a lifetime commitment.

If you were not brought up by your parents, it is often difficult to work through the feelings attached to this feeling of loss or abandonment. At a young age it is easy to believe that somehow you may have been the cause of them going away, even as a result of death. It is important to work through these emotions and release any negative feelings about your childhood to help you fully develop your potential and gain self-confidence. Work through the exercises in Chapter 3, Forgive and Forget, to let go of all feelings of guilt or anger to allow you to fully open up your heart to others.

Reliance

During your childhood years you were reliant on your parents, or a responsible adult, for all of life's necessities – maintenance of your physical body, shaping of your mind and spirit. You will probably have derived some habits, attitudes and beliefs from each of your parents, biological or not. Depending on where you are in the pecking order – eldest, youngest or in between – your parents' attitudes about raising children probably changed over the years, so what some of your siblings may have learned may not be the same as what you learned. It was certainly true in my family, where I am the youngest of 3 girls by twelve years and the eldest is 16 years older than me. We span different generational attitudes, and therefore are quite different from each other. If you are an only child you may rely even more on your parents for not only the guidance and necessities, but also for companionship. In your later years, you may have to reverse roles and look after them.

Independent thought

As you develop and have more life experiences – visiting
friends' homes, travelling to different towns or cities, meeting
people from different backgrounds – you begin to see the
contrasts or differences between what you have learned and
what other people have experienced. Over time this may cause
you to question some of the things you learned and open up
your mind to a broader perspective. Each generation has its
own level of advancement by stretching beyond what people
had been taught. When I was growing up there were no
computers. Now 5-year-olds are able to get information on
their own. This is a staggering advancement of opportunities
in under 50 years, yet those schooled in old ways may never
be open minded enough to even try it!

Rebellion

At some stage in your teenage years, if you were like most
teenagers, you went through a period of rebellion, seeing how
far you could push the boundaries that were set by your
parents. Some of you may have started questioning things at
an early age or never felt a need to rebel at all, but usually
there is a moment when you start to question the things
you have learned. This is a normal part of development
and helps you to find your own footing – trying things out
and testing your own moral values as you begin to make
your own decisions. Depending on your own particular
family structure and how your parents were on the strict–
lenient scale, you may have been encouraged to present
your own viewpoint or you may have never been allowed
to challenge your parents' viewpoints. Again, this can have
a dramatic impact on how you view the world today

and can impact on how you currently relate to figures of authority.

Acceptance

There are many positive traits and skills that you have learned from your parents that have become part of your character. As you get older and gain perspective, you are more able to accept your parents for the good things they have brought to your life. As in any relationship, there will be things that you find difficult about your relationship with your parents that can get in the way of forming a close relationship with them throughout your life. By letting go of some of the learned childhood behaviour patterns, you can better relate to your parents on an equal footing.

Role reversal

As you get older and begin to reverse roles with your parents, it is important to make peace with them for all that has passed. Whether you take on these responsibilities begrudgingly or with love will make an enormous difference. Chapter 3, Forgive and Forget, can help you to release pent-up feelings.

Whatever your belief system, many of the beliefs and attitudes that you have today are a result of your parents' influence in your formative years. For some it can be the model of expectation of what their life will be like in the future; indeed, many people follow in their parents' or role model's footsteps, and it is easy to see why. Others who have had a broader perspective may seek to move on from their parents' beliefs. And still others, having had a more negative upbringing, may use it as an example of what they don't want. In all cases it is a starting point from which to explore the universe.

Let's take a look at the things that you learned from your parents or those that looked after you, when you were young. This is not intended to be an emotional exercise, but do not be surprised at what you may write. Just think about the first things that come to mind and try not to make any judgements about the answers. This is just a starting point to see where some of your traits may have developed.

Self-confidence

- What were you told that you did well?
- What were you told that you did badly?
- How was your physical appearance viewed?
- Were you encouraged to communicate your thoughts and feelings?
- Were you encouraged to try new things?
- What were you encouraged to do in the future?

Values

- What household chores were you made to do each day?
- What values did you learn about money?
- Were you brought up with any formal religious training or spiritual guidance?
- How were the relationships of those around you?
- Was education important in your family?
- Were you encouraged to try things again that you failed at?

Take a few minutes to review your answers and look at how each answer makes you feel now, in the moment. If you find that you have strong reactions to any of the answers, such as feelings of anger, sadness or regret, these are areas to tackle in the exercises in Chapter 3, Forgive and Forget. It is by releasing these deep-rooted feelings from your childhood that you can de-junk some attitudes and beliefs about your abilities and see yourself for who you are right now.

What we learned through our education

Your formal education is your first true separation from your parents, where you learn the intellectual skills that you still use each and every day. It is also the time when you first learn to stand on your own and make choices. You make friends, develop social skills and begin to discover your own moral code of what is right and wrong.

The individual experiences that you had in school have helped to shape your attitude about your abilities. If you were encouraged to develop your natural gifts and to persevere with those areas that you may have found challenging, you probably gained a great deal from your schooling that continues to serve you well. Once you know that you have the ability to learn new things, you develop the self-confidence to try new and more challenging areas of interest. Positive learning experiences encourage you to continue to show interest in learning new things. Good students usually remain good students throughout all of their educational training, and in later life are more confident in pursuing new challenges.

Conversely, negative early learning experiences can affect your attitude towards learning new things on an on-going basis. Just as positive reinforcement from teachers or family can help you to achieve all that you can, negative reinforcement can lower your self-esteem and lessen your own expectations of your abilities. If you don't think you are clever enough to do something, unfortunately, you don't bother trying, when often it just takes a different method of learning to gain competence in the skill.

Negative learning experiences do not reflect your intellect! Boredom, lack of direction or unsuitable teaching methods all impact on how well you did at school. We all have different ways of processing information. Some people are very visual and need to see things in a graphic manner to be able fully to understand. Other people are more logical, and need to have facts and figures to understand. Some people need to listen to something to have it really sink in and others need to write things down to be able to learn them. In other words, not everyone fits into the system.

Looking back at your educational experience can act as a refresher, helping you to remember some of the skills that you learned early on. It can also help you to realize that you have absorbed some negative beliefs about your capabilities that have prevented you from reaching your maximum potential. It's never too late to learn new skills that you may not have succeeded at in the past. Once you are able to understand how you best learn new information, you can tackle any new learning experience. In Chapter 5, Building on Your Success, you will learn how to make the most of your areas of strength and how to incorporate those skills into all areas of your life.

- Did you enjoy your educational experience?
- Were you a good student?
- What were your favourite subjects?
- What were your least favourite subjects?
- What skills do you still use that you learned at school?
- What were your career goals when you finished your schooling?

- Did you achieve them?
- How do you most easily learn new things (i.e. reading, watching a demonstration, listening to someone)?

In reviewing your answers, look at the areas where you felt limited by the educational system, your own expectations or expectations of teachers and family. If you feel that you have been held back as a result of your educational experiences, it's never too late to do something about it. Try to gain some understanding from your positive learning experiences as to the best way that you process information and seek out educational experiences that will enable you to learn things the best way for you. There are many outstanding part-time courses to help you gain many basic and advanced skills.

What we learned from our friends

As the old saying goes, you can't choose your family, but you can choose your friends. Over time, friends will come and go, but for the time they were in your life they were an important part of your development. Your friends provide companionship, inspiration and an important outlet to enable you to express your inner feelings. Friends are often there to help you work out problems and to give you another perspective on things that are happening in your life. When you look back at the friendships you have developed throughout your life, you will probably find that specific friends came into your life just when you needed them!

At an early age, your parents put you together with other children your own age to socialize. They were probably your cousins or children of your parents' friends. If you played with children slightly older than you, they were probably instrumental in helping you to learn the ropes, as we often model our own behaviour on those we look up to.

As you leave your home to go to school, you begin to develop your own friendships. Most probably your school friends lived close by in your neighbourhood or were members of your class. Your siblings could also be classified as your friends, especially if you are close in age. In all cases, you had things in common. You may still have a relationship with friends you met at this time in your life when dramatic growth occurred. Most likely you shared many intimate details about your personal thoughts and activities with these friends.

As you get older, you are most likely to make friends as a result of a common interest. This could be through your work, neighbours, members of a religious organization, children, or any special interest that you may have. These types of friendships often enable you to learn new things, keep your mind stimulated and help you to stay connected to the world outside of your immediate surroundings.

In some cases, you may acquire friends through a relationship with others, such as your spouse or partner's friends. Anyone that you choose to spend time with will have an influence on your life. In the case of acquired friends, you may find that you have less in common with them than friends you developed on your own.

What have you learned about yourself and your relationships with others through the friendships you have developed? When answering these questions, go back as far as you can remember and think about all of the friends that have entered your life.

- What do you expect from your friends?
- Which friends do you trust with your confidences?

- Which friends give you good advice?
- Which friends motivate you to try new things?
- Which friends can you rely on?
- Which friends let you down?
- In what ways have you been a good friend?
- Have you fallen out with any of your friends?
- Who is your best friend? Why?

When you look at your answers, you will be able to appreciate how much your friends bring to your life. You will also feel how much it warms your heart just thinking about your friends. If you have lost touch with friends who have been meaningful in your life, this is a great opportunity to take some time to track them down. It is easier than ever by searching the Internet.

True friendship is about giving without any strings attached. It is easy to take friendships for granted or to place your values on those of your friends. Look at your answers to the questions above and see if you are holding on to any emotional baggage about friends you currently have or have had in the past.

By releasing old hurts, you accept that each of us is human and prone to make mistakes. Try any of the release exercises in Chapter 3 to feel better in an instant.

What we learned from our culture

It is often very comforting to fit into a group. Being with people who share similar experiences can feel safe and non-threatening. As an individual, you probably fit into many different groups. On the grand scale, you share with human beings the properties of being in a physical body on earth.

You belong to a group of people who live in the same country. You live in a geographic region that shares similar accents, or weather, and you may live in an area with many families from similar ethnic backgrounds. Each group of which you are a member can also influence your attitudes and beliefs. To challenge the attitudes and beliefs of the group can set you apart.

Cultural values, both ethnic and national, often dictate social behaviour. Your choice of suitable marriage partner and even whom you date can be as a result of the cultural practices of where you live and your ethnic background. Family or peer pressure can make it difficult to make your own decisions based on how you feel, rather than what you were taught. The difference between cultures can be massive, with each culture having its own set of social values. In many countries the cost of questioning national or ethnic values can be devastating. You can be an outcast or worse. However, it is often as a result of questioning these cultural 'rules' that social change occurs. Many personal freedoms have been gained by questioning existing values.

You have probably heard of and even experienced the term 'collective consciousness'. It usually applies to a large group of people who are together for a common purpose and who feel a sense of shared feelings with the entire gathering. It can happen at a concert, a wedding, or even by watching a sporting event on television where people are together for the same purpose. Inhabitants of a country also have a collective consciousness with other people who live in the same country. The ethos and attitudes of that particular country are imbedded in all aspects of the culture and it is necessary to adopt these attitudes in order to 'fit in'. It is often said that the English are reserved, or the Australians are enthusiastic, and although these are stereotypical, there are events in the history of each country that shape the attitudes of future generations.

As an American living in England and married to an Englishman, I find many cultural differences between the United States and England. As an observer, it is easier to see how these cultural differences may impact on the country as a whole. In my work dealing with people's hoarding habits in the UK, I often see the impact of rationing in England during WWII. Generations of people were taught never to throw anything away because it might come in handy some day. As a result of this cultural attitude, millions of Brits hold on to things they don't want or like and will never use simply out of fear or guilt about breaking a social 'norm'. Although there may be many cultural attitudes that are worth practicing, there are obviously many other cultural attitudes that you have the choice to reject.

Your ethnic background also shapes your attitudes and beliefs. These attitudes and beliefs are taught to you through your family and, in many cases, through living in an area with families of similar ethnic backgrounds. If your family is religious, then your religious education would also impact on your ethnic cultural beliefs. While you were still living in your family home, it may have been difficult to question these practices and beliefs.

The influences around you can often make it difficult for you to stand on your own two feet. If you are strong willed, or have a deep sense of what feels right and wrong for you, it may have been easier for you to stand up for your own personal beliefs, even amid the pressure of the group. However, it is possible for the need to belong or the need for approval to keep you from challenging any beliefs that you don't agree with.

Take a look at the things that you learned from your

culture and ethnic background to see how they influence your thoughts and actions in the present moment.

- What did your cultural upbringing teach you about voicing your opinion?
- Did your cultural upbringing influence your choice of relationships?
- Do you disagree with any of the cultural beliefs you were taught?
- Were you encouraged to learn more about different cultures?
- Did your cultural or ethnic background influence your choice of career?
- How did your cultural background influence your eating habits?
- Did your cultural background influence your choice of friends?
- What does your ethnic background mean to you?

Unwanted cultural beliefs are often the most difficult to release because of the pressures that may be placed on you by those around you. It is very difficult to stand out from the pack. Distancing yourself from the situation can give you perspective and allow you to understand your feelings without undue influence.

Look at some of the cultural beliefs that you take issue with and try some of the methods in Chapter 6, Speak Up, to enable you to voice your opinion and feel comfortable with your decisions.

What we learned from our faith

You don't have to practise a particular religion, or even any religion at all, to have faith. By definition, faith is an inner-knowing or confident belief in the truth, value or trustworthiness of people, ideas and situations. This type of faith often comes from the experiences that you have had during your lifetime. You have faith that when you turn on the tap, water will flow because, except perhaps for the rare occasion, water flows when you turn on the tap. You may have faith in certain people because in the past they have always been there when you needed them. Hopefully, you have developed faith in your own abilities that gives you the self-confidence to go after many of the things you want out of life.

Spiritual faith is a belief that does not rely on logical proof or explanation, and again does not need to be consigned to any particular religion. Anyone who believes that there is a greater force other than our physical being on earth has spiritual faith. You do not have to participate in organized religion to be a spiritual person.

As a child, you were probably given some spiritual guidance by your parents. This may have involved religious training or going to a place of worship. It may, alternatively, have taken the form of a more generalized, non-sectarian view of God or a higher source of energy. You may have been taught to give thanks at meals, or to say your prayers at the end of the day, or moral guidance about what is right and wrong.

When you leave your family home, you are more likely to begin to take your own decisions on spiritual practice. You may choose to study other spiritual beliefs, be less stringent in the practice of your faith, or question the things you were taught. It is natural to explore your own feelings about your relationship with the universe and God. The more life experiences that you can't understand or find answers to, the more likely you are to look for the answers in a spiritual way. During different phases of your life, your connection with your faith may alter.

You have probably learned many positive and comforting things over the years.

At some time in your life you may also have had a loss of faith. This could mean a loss of faith in your own abilities, or a loss of a spiritual connection when you feel that your faith let you down. A loss of faith generally makes you feel bad physically and emotionally – a clear indication that thinking in a negative way does not serve your goals and desires. Any blame that you assign, to yourself or to others, makes you feel bad and keeps you reliving the situation.

Whatever your spiritual beliefs may be, looking at the things that you learned as a result of your spiritual practice can enable you to choose the elements that make you feel connected with a higher source of energy.

- Are you a spiritual person?
- Did you learn about religious practices when you were growing up?
- Do you currently participate in religious practice?
- Are you tolerant of other people's faith?
- When was the last time you felt a spiritual connection?
- What do you have faith in (people, ideas, objects)?
- Have you ever lost faith? Why?
- List the ways your faith has impacted on your life.

No matter what your religious beliefs may be, when you are able to feel a higher spiritual connection with the universe, you will never feel alone. If you have lost your faith, spend some quiet time communing with nature to enable you to see beauty and wonder every day that was not created by man.

Look at all the events in your life that have enabled you to feel a spiritual connection and try to incorporate them into your daily life. By showing appreciation each day for what you have, you will feel the wonderful effects of faith in action.

What I learned from my life experience

Your life experiences are all the things that have occurred in your life so far. Every day you have many routine experiences that are not particularly memorable but help you to refine your likes and dislikes. You might have always travelled to work by bus, but through experience you find that you actually prefer to travel by train. These daily experiences help you to see the contrast between the choices that are available.

The more memorable life experiences are the ones that you tend to hold on to. Some of your memorable experiences will be treasured memories that make you feel good when you think about them. Other memories that you may hold on to can be of unpleasant experiences in the past which continue to influence your life. It is only by releasing these negative experiences from cluttering your mind that you will be able to move on and begin to feel better about yourself. The following story shows how negative experiences can impact on all areas of your life and limit your potential for experiencing new things.

I recently had a conversation with a close girlfriend who has had some tough circumstances to deal with over the last ten years. She is very attractive and intelligent and has been successful at many things she has attempted, yet she knocks herself down at every opportunity. She always apologizes about never looking good enough, or cooking well enough when in actuality, she always is exceptionally well put together, is a terrific cook and has exquisite taste. She has experienced great loss in her romantic life through the death of two partners, and struggles financially to live a lifestyle that she finds comfortable. She has been unable to get out from under the weight of her last ten years of disappointments.

On this occasion, we had planned to go to a friend's birthday drinks, but she called to say she was under the weather. A few days later I called to see how she was to find that she was quite down and felt lacking in both energy and enthusiasm. Wanting to help, based on my experiences with helping people though times of life changes, I suggested to her that she should try to do a little something that made her feel better – right then and there – because by feeling even a bit better, you raise your vibration. I suggested some music, a favourite DVD, a walk in the park or even a soak in the tub with some appropriate oils, to make her feel a bit better about herself. If you feel better you are more optimistic and are more likely to have more positive thoughts – it gets the juices flowing.

I was surprised by her answer. My friend got quite emotional and told me that she felt she had the right to feel down whenever she wanted to. She did not believe that it was possible to be 'up' all the time. I agreed that it was probably not possible to be up all the time, but if you were given the choice between feeling up and feeling down, surely you would want to feel up. She vehemently fought for her right to feel bad and felt that I was judging her for being unhappy.

I felt badly about upsetting my friend – she had not asked for my advice, and I should not have given it. I genuinely wanted to help and felt that the advice was so obvious that it could hardly be contentious. Yet sometimes, feeling bad is what you have done for so long that you close your mind to believing that things can get better. The next day she left a message on my answering machine saying that she was sorry for getting so angry. After our phone call something prompted her to pick up a book that advised exactly the same thing and it made a lot of sense. The more times you have had a hurtful life experience, the longer it can take you to get out of the habit of expecting it to happen again.

Sometimes it is easy to get into the habit of anticipating the outcome of an experience based on your past experiences of the same nature. A good example is a child who gets bitten by a dog. In all likelihood, the next time this child sees a dog, he will probably be fearful that the dog will bite him again. If the same child has had lots of experience with dogs and has only been bitten this one time, the child might be less fearful of the dog because his past experiences were of a positive nature.

The same is true in all areas of your life. If you have had a positive experience in a relationship, job or an achievement, the next time you want a new job or to enter into a new relationship or to come up with a new idea, your life experience will have taught you that you are likely to succeed at it because you have in the past. If you have had a negative experience, you may prejudge future experiences based on the past. Without giving the new experience a chance, you will always limit your potential enjoyment.

Everyone can identify with having to go to the doctor or dentist and really not looking forward to it because you anticipate that it will be an unpleasant experience. The truth is that it is most often over in a short period of time and you are able to forget about it and move on. Often, the anticipation is much worse than the actual experience. And even when the experience is unpleasant – perhaps giving birth is a good example – the benefits so outweigh the limited duration of unpleasantness that it is always worth the effort. In other words, if we have an unpleasant experience, it doesn't always mean that future similar experiences will be unpleasant. Letting go of the memory can enable you to judge new experiences with an open mind.

Let's explore some of the things you learned as a result of the experiences you have had so far. Try to base your answers on all the feedback you have had from the combination of your experiences rather than from one in particular.

- What things are you good at?
- What things do you most enjoy doing?
- What people/things are most important to you?
- What areas of your life need improving?
- What makes you feel confident?
- What makes you feel insecure?
- What has disappointed you?
- Is there anything that has happened in your life that prevents you from experiencing new things?

During your lifetime the experiences that you have will formulate your future choices. Good experiences will encourage you to choose similar types of experience in the future. Looking at past positive experiences can help you make more productive decisions in all areas of your life. Use this information to help you plan career moves, explore new relationships and create situations that make you feel at your best.

You will also have had some less pleasant experiences that don't have to hold you back. Looking at them is the best way to conquer them. Given a second opportunity, what would you change if you had to go through it all over again? Once you have learned the lesson from the experience, you can let it go and move on. All of the exercises in Chapter 2, What Your Habits Say About You, are designed to help rid you of negative mind junk and give you the confidence to try things again.

What does it all mean?

All the things you have learned in the past have shaped your life decisions. The older you get, the more life experiences you have, and the more you should be able to refine your attitudes and decisions to reflect what you want in the current moment, rather than what you wanted in the past. Like cleaning out a bookshelf and getting rid of books that no longer reflect your interests or requirements, you need to give the things you have learned a good look to be certain that you still believe them. The more you experience, the more you are subject to change your views and opinions. Stubborn people, who hold on to old beliefs without continuing to question them, have closed minds.

You have learned things from many sources; some more in-fluential than others. Certainly, your early childhood develop-ment provides some of the most ingrained values and choices in your character. The more independent and questioning your nature, the more likely you are to have made your own choices as soon as you were old enough. Those with a more accepting nature, or who lived with or near their parents for a longer time, may accept and never question things they were taught and, as long as that feels good, it is the right choice. All that matters is that you feel good about what you are doing and things will fall into place. Unfortunately, there are many who place the blame for all of their life's woes on their parents, and can hold on to this anger for a lifetime. It doesn't feel good and it doesn't move you on.

Free will

The good news is that you have free will to make different choices each and every day. You can throw all of your old beliefs out the window and try something different. You can choose to see the good in every situation and feel the difference in how it makes you feel. You can live in the present moment and use all of your senses to enjoy every experience that you have in the course of the day and see how much better it feels thinking about and giving your best effort to everything you do. One small positive action can change everything about the day. You can change an attitude, belief, the way you feel, a relationship, a job or just about anything, simply by looking for ways to do it.

Everything you have written down about the things you've learned so far is a part of your history. These things have made you who you are today. Who you are later this evening, tomorrow afternoon or in forty years' time, will solely depend on the choices you make in the future. You have the free will to accept or reject any future experience starting this moment. You have the choice to stop thinking about things that you cannot change from the past, but take immediate steps to change the future.

The way to continuously grow and keep a youthful spirit throughout your lifetime is to continue to have the desire to experience new things. As soon as you abandon the desire for living, you lose your energy and will to go on. Sadly, many elderly people give up on themselves far too early. With medical advancements in many parts of the world, the average life expectancy continues to rise and you are more likely to get there with the desire to do it. Wouldn't it be great to live a life filled with fun and adventure for as long as you desire it to go on?

I would like you to go back to the last exercise, look at all of your answers and do two things. The first is to mark a giant tick next to those things that have worked for you and you still believe are beneficial in your life. I bet you have found many beliefs that you have forgotten about over the years. Use this exercise as a reminder to focus on these positive elements of your character and use them to their highest advantage. Start a new page entitled 'Positive Beliefs and Attitudes that Work for me.' Keep it in a place that you can easily see whenever you need an extra boost.

After you have finished with the things you still value as a result of your life experiences to date, go through the remaining attitudes and beliefs that you have found to be untrue or no longer believe in. You may have been told that you were not clever enough to do something only to find you are brilliant at it! Call upon your inner knowing to help you in this, as some of the things that you learned may be very hurtful and deep down inside you know they are not true. Reach down to let go of false illusions and acknowledge your own self-worth. Deep down inside, you really know that you are a good person with unique special things about you. Let them out!

2.

What Your Habits Say About You

Most people learn things most easily through repetition. From the time you are an infant and on a particular feeding schedule, to learning your alphabet when you first enter school, you were taught things over and over again on a daily basis until you learned the routine. Six weeks of consistent practice on a daily basis is all it takes for most people to get into a routine or habit, or to learn a concept or idea. If you are given positive reinforcement, such as a gold star from your teacher, a treat from your parents, or words of praise, you are more likely to learn quickly and associate that habit with something that is good. Sometimes you can also learn a habit or routine through negative reinforcement, meaning that rather than getting praise for doing something well, you got punishment if you didn't do something well. You may have still learned the routine, but may associate that routine with something negative. Either way you have developed a habit, and once it becomes imbedded into your deeper consciousness, it becomes a part of what you do without having to really think about it. The longer that you have a habit or routine, the more difficult it can be to break; therefore, habits that are developed in childhood often stick with you the longest.

The nature of a habit is that you don't think about it, so you remove your awareness from the situation. Even good habits can benefit from a conscious awareness of what you are doing in the moment. A good example of this is brushing your teeth. You may remember from early childhood that you need to brush your teeth two or three times a day and continue that practice today as a matter of habit. However, it is not just about brushing your teeth; it is about how you brush your teeth – whether you pay attention to all areas of your mouth. Bringing your awareness to each experience will ensure that you know what you are doing and make the choice from a position of awareness rather than habit.

The following are areas we often take for granted or do out of habit, and may not get our full attention. See which areas need more of your attention.

- Personal hygiene
- Health
- Eating and drinking habits
- Housekeeping
- Loved ones
- Appearance
- Important dates

Sometimes it takes a negative experience to jolt you into realizing that you have actually developed a habit and have stopped paying attention to something that you do routinely. An illness indicates that you need to pay more attention to your body. A huge credit card bill means that you have to start to pay attention to your spending. If you stop paying close attention to the cleanliness of your house, for example, and don't really look into the nooks and crannies, you are likely to be jolted into awareness by having problems with insects, nasty smells or rodents. If you habitually cross the street in the same way every day and don't even notice that there are road works in place, a near miss can jolt you into a sense of awareness. The fact that most traffic accidents occur within a mile of your own home can be in part due to the route becoming so routine that you stop paying attention. Whenever you stop paying attention to things, they can easily get out of control without your noticing.

If you choose to ignore the warning, you may continue having near misses or warning experiences that try to alert you to what is going on. If you fail to take positive, constructive action to change the situation it can have more serious implications. For example, I have seen people who live in cluttered homes who will trip over something or injure themselves as a result of having too many things. If they use this experience to get rid of stuff and make more space so that it won't happen again, the negative experience brought their attention to the state of their home and they could take positive action to fix it. If they still don't see the problem, it may happen again and again, until something more serious happens to get their attention. All of your experiences are there to guide you, and whenever you are aware, you have freedom of choice to do something to change the experience.

Look at the following situations and see if you have been ignoring some indications that have developed bad habits.

- More than one person has offered you advice about a habit of yours
- You have recurring health issues
- You never have enough money to pay the bills
- You find it difficult to fall asleep
- You are lacking in energy.

Learn from your good habits

Most of us can identify our good and bad habits, even if we don't acknowledge them often. Good habits, in general, make you feel good as they generally lead to a positive and desirable outcome. Because they are habits, however, we often forget to pay attention to them and look at them as achievements. Every success you have achieved to date in your personal and professional life comes not from luck, but from good habits, attitudes and beliefs that you have learned through all your life experiences. Your kindness, generosity, loving nature, curiosity, intelligence, humour, creativity, enthusiasm, perseverance and all that is positive about you comes from the positive and wonderful things you have learned through all of your experiences and that continue to serve you well. Taking the time to look at your many good habits can teach you to focus on your strengths rather than your failings.

Achievements are things that made you feel special as a result of having accomplished them. Anything that is special is memorable and can stay with you for your entire lifetime. Achievements do not have to be huge leaps forward. Even a small movement forward can still be monumental to you. Look at the many athletic records that are held for years and years and when finally beaten, it is only by a fraction of a second. Or look at someone who has suffered a debilitating illness and learns how to take a step. Any small step forward is an achievement and deserves to be recognized and appreciated. It really helps to boost your self-confidence, which enables you to believe you can reach for even higher goals.

Looking back at your past achievements from as far back as you can remember can help to remind you of some of the things about yourself that you may have forgotten as you move forward in time. You may have excelled at reading as a child, yet now you never get a chance to sit down with a good book. Your achievements show examples of how your focused energy or attention on the object of your desire helps you to get it! Make a list of all of your achievements and think back to the good habits that got you there. Try to incorporate them more into your daily routines.

Every day you do things that are wonderful as a matter of habit, and I bet you never acknowledge them in your own self. All too often, we look towards other people to give us our sense of self-worth. We want our family and employers to appreciate our actions, when often we don't appreciate them ourselves. Until you are able to accept your own validation for things you know you have done well, your security and well-being will always depend on others' approval. The more you are able to see your accomplishments on a daily basis, the stronger, happier and more self-reliant you will become. As soon as you have the realization that you are in charge of every choice you make, and as a result responsible for every action you take, you will stop blaming others for your current circumstances. Most importantly, it feels good to feel good about yourself. Feeling good is contagious. It uplifts everyone around you and raises the vibration so that your environment reflects your positive attitude.

Starting today, at the end of each day, keep a notebook by the side of your bed. Take a few minutes at bedtime to think about everything you did that made you or others feel good today and give thanks for all that you achieved. Showing appreciation opens up your heart and asks the universe for more of the same! Try it out and see what happens.

Bad habits feel bad

Bad habits, in general, make you feel bad. You can relate to the physically bad feeling of a hangover or smoking too many cigarettes or not getting enough sleep or exercise because it is easy to see the cause and effect of your actions. Because bad habits make you feel bad, and it is difficult to ignore something that makes you feel bad, it is easy to spend a lot of time thinking or worrying about them. However, the bad feeling is intended to get your attention and cause you to take action to make yourself feel better. For example, you may give up drinking for a while after a major spree, but it is easy to slip back into the bad habit as there is the comfort factor of doing something that you have done before. It is often easier to go out and do what your friends do and drink too much, or to smoke cigarettes because it gives you something to do with your hands in a social situation, than to find something to replace that behaviour.

Bad habits can also affect you on the emotional level by making you feel guilty, angry or unhappy. Bad habits can give you instant gratification in the moment and may make you feel good, but when you have taken the decision to do something that you know is not good for you, your emotions, or inner guidance system, let you know that what you are doing is not for your highest good. If you begin to slip into old bad habits, these feelings of disappointment in yourself can lead to depression and lack of self-esteem. They can also lead to lack of mental clarity. If you find yourself on an emotional roller coaster, what you are doing or thinking at that moment does not benefit your ultimate goals.

Another effect of bad habits is that you may get negative feedback or negative attention as a result of them. Negative social habits such as drinking too much and causing a nuisance, or smoking in public places, can often draw a negative response from a larger audience. If you take on board the fact that lots of people think that your habit is inappropriate, you may come to the conclusion that they are correct and choose to change it based on the cumulative negative reactions to your habit or behaviour. If as a result of your bad habit you get attention, it may be that you like the attention, whether it is good attention or bad attention, and continue to practise the habit. Although bad attention doesn't feel good in the long run, you might just want to be noticed or try out new things.

The more time you spend with people, the more likely they are to get to see a lot of your habits and practices. Your own good habits help to raise the standards of those around you as you always lead by your own example. Other people's habits provide the contrast for you to determine whether your habits are the best choice for you. Being open minded and looking at new possibilities enables you to shed old routines for ones that work better.

Your habits affect those around you

On both a personal and professional level, all of your habits affect those around you. Your habits have a direct result on the attitudes and habits of your children, as your parents influenced many of your own habits. Your habits influence your pets' habits, as they will always be reliant on you to be looking after their best interests. Your habits influence those you work with, both in judging your contribution to the organization and in your ability to lead others or to be a reliable part of the team. Your habits can also influence how you are treated in the corner shop, or how you treat others when you take control of a car. Each and every action you take causes a reaction.

You will most likely know how your habits affect others by the feedback you receive from them. Feedback can be written, verbal and, more often than not, non-verbal, by body language or gestures. If you are not paying attention to people around you and are off in your own little world, unless it is direct feedback, like the written or spoken word, it can be easy to miss. In the case of any feedback, it can also be easy to misinterpret, as your emotional or physical attachment to your habit often gets in the way of looking at things objectively.

Feedback is a mechanism that is intended to bring your awareness to the situation so that you view it from a different perspective. If you listen to the feedback when it is offered, you can then judge whether you agree with it or not. The esteem in which you hold the person who has given you the feedback is often a good way of initially judging how much you value their opinion. If someone has usually given you good advice and now offers you feedback, it is probably something you are willing to consider. You may not consider other people's feedback important at all, so it is always a matter of judging whom you are going to listen to!

Often times it takes repeated feedback in order for you to come to the realization that you must pay more attention to the situation. If it happens once, sit up and take notice. If it happens twice, it is time to give the matter serious consideration. And I always believe that when things happen three times, they are always true! When the same feedback is received from many different sources, it is time to take action. It is sometimes very difficult to open your mind up and accept new input, but it always makes you a more informed,

interesting and ever-growing individual discovering more and
more about yourself through every experience.

How other people's bad habits can affect you

The more intimate your relationship, the more your personal
habits are likely to impact on others close to you. The more
time you spend with people in a wide array of circumstances,
the more you are able to see their strengths and weaknesses.
Because other people's habits may differ from your own way
of thinking, it is easy to point out the differences, as partners
could easily point out the areas in which your habits differ
from theirs. If you let the differences in another's habits
become the focus of your attention, it can make you feel
bad and probably doesn't change their habit. With all close
relationships, individual habits in some area of your life will
probably clash and cause conflict.

Think about an example of one partner in a relationship
who always throws their clothes on the floor each night. He
or she might prefer to use the time to read the newspaper or
watch television in order to relax, and to him or her, the
world will not come to an end if their clothes are on the floor.
The truth is, they are right; the world won't come to an end
based on this bad habit. The fact that the clothes may get
wrinkled and have to be laundered more often, or that it may
not look very nice or it may be unpleasant for the next person
who has to share that space is probably something they don't
really think about, and if it is more important to you than it
is to your partner, you must work out a compromise.

Now take the same set of circumstances and add some
children to the picture.

One partner throws their clothes on the floor every night

and it may be that your children come into the bedroom every night and see this. The other partner is upset because this habit all of a sudden takes on a bit more importance, as you are now showing your children by your behaviour that this is an acceptable way of behaving. Any action will have different consequences in different situations.

Living with other people's habits

In reality, you can't change anyone's habits or change anyone's priorities, but you can learn to control your reactions to them. In the end, it is up to each individual to set his or her own value system. What is important to you may not be important to someone else, so to him or her, their habit is insignificant as they may have higher priorities. All relationships involve compromise, and again it is always a matter of degree that helps you to decide which things are worth pointing out and which are simply easier to deal with on your own. As we often cling to our old habits, there are always emotions involved. It is interesting to note that it is often easier to see other people's faults rather than your own. It is also said that others' faults are a reflection of your own. Is it true in your case?

If someone else's habit makes you feel bad as a result of that habit, there are several choices you can make:

- You can decide that the habit, on the grand scale of it all, isn't really that important, and choose to ignore it.
- You don't let the habit bother you, and you do whatever you have to do to make the situation more pleasant for you. Always remember that you are

doing this to make yourself feel better, not to prove a point. In this case, proving a point is a negative reaction and doesn't make you feel good. By doing it with an open heart you both benefit from the experience. Whereas it may not ever bring the other person's awareness to the problem, it also won't ruin a relationship over something that may not be significant.

- You can argue on a matter of principle that their behaviour isn't fair according to your standards. This probably won't make you feel very good and can be a continual source of unpleasantness in your relationship. Most importantly, who says your standards are correct? Sometimes, the more you try to impose your standards on others, the more they stick firmly to their own principles. It is a matter of territory. Everyone has stubborn traits.

Principles and strong opinions

Habits that we believe strongly in may become principles and are deeply ingrained in our characters. Although you think of most people's principles as being their moral and ethical code, it is equally possible to develop other principles based on habits.

It is good to express your convictions, but it can close your mind to other opinions and experiences that do not fit into your way of thinking and you may miss out on many opportunities and experiences.

Sometimes we use general principles to justify our behaviour. We might justify the use of our freedom of speech by saying exactly what is on our mind under any circumstances. We might justify our right to smoke as a personal liberty allowing us to take choices about our own body. While you do have these rights and they are good principles when fighting about things you truly believe in, can you really fight for something that you know is going to hurt you or others? Sometimes it is important to take other people's feelings or rights into account when you take a stand and think deeply about your decision.

If you don't try something you will never know the answer. When you continue to test your principles to see if they still hold true in all situations, they are more meaningful as they stand the test of time. Each experience that you have adds to the information you store about similar experiences you have had before, in order for you to be able to compare them to refine your opinion. If you stop having new experiences, you deny that life moves on and there are advancements that may benefit you. When you test a new experience, you always have the right to choose whether it works for you or not. The key is to allow yourself an open mind and judge fairly. Sometimes it takes a while to get used to something new and you may have to try it a few times to feel comfortable. The benefit is that you may enjoy the experience and learn something new in the process. And even if you don't like it, it may serve to strengthen your belief in the principles that continue to work for you.

De-Junking unwanted habits

As with anything in life, it is all about putting things into context. By looking at the degree that your habits impact on your life, you are able to determine how important they really are. We are often our own worst critics. It is easy to set unrealistic goals and targets as the pressures of daily living often take up much more time that you expect. Everything in life is about achieving a balance. For every action, there is an equal and an opposite reaction, and there are always two sides to the same coin. When you assess your current habits, it is important to see where they are on the scale of acceptable behaviour for you and those around you. How your habits and behaviour make you feel is the best indicator to make these judgements. Habits on either end of the spectrum are extreme, and whether they are extremely good or extremely bad, extreme behaviour and habits often need to be moderated to enable you to feel your best.

As you are all individuals at different stages of your own personal development and self-awareness, in some areas of your life you might take comfort in some of your habits and routines, as everything is predictable. If it feels good, and you are doing what you want, continuing in the same routines may be right for you in the present moment. However, if you always wish you could do something else and it is the fear of trying something different that is stopping you, the effects of regret are far more negative and long lasting than trying something and not liking it or not being good at it.

As you develop your confidence by changing small, insignificant habits, like where you do your shopping, or the route you take to work, it broadens your perspective to try more new experiences. If you have always had a holiday with your parents/partners/friends or you always go to the same destination, you might find you are ready to do that differently. Small successful changes of habit keep broadening your perspective and giving you the confidence to keep trying and testing out new ideas.

In order to de-junk your mind of existing habits, it is important to focus on the positive routines that you would like to develop. By assessing where you are in the present moment, you have a starting point and know where you need to improve. Assessing your habits in an open way allows you to explore new avenues in areas that have not worked for you in the past. The following areas highlight many common habits and illustrate how tendencies on either end of the spectrum make it difficult to achieve balance in your life. In all cases, setting your goals towards achieving the mid-range of the spectrum will help you break your existing habits.

Let's look at some of the most common habits or tendencies and see where you think you fit in on the scale. We all need a starting point, to know where we are. Assessing your habits in an honest and open way allows you to explore new avenues in areas that have not worked for you in the past. For the first part of the exercise, look at your life over the period of the last few months and take into account all of the experiences you have had during this time. If there were exceptional circumstances, try to rule them out and look at your most typical or average tendencies during that time.

Lazy —————————— *Relaxed* —————————— *Driven*

The one thing these habits have in common is motivation. On the laziness end of the spectrum, you are lacking motivation or desire to go out into the world and get what you want. On the other end of the spectrum, you may be so busy getting what you want, that you forget that your body needs time to relax and enjoy the fruits of your labours. Both habits come from your desires in the moment.

Everyone may go through a period of exhibiting one tendency or another. In your youth, without being focused on what you wanted, as you had not yet had enough experience to know, you may have been lazier, with your desires more recreational and social. When you try to make your mark on the world through your career, you are so focused on what you want that you rule out so many potential experiences that could lead you in another direction which, indeed, may be an even better choice for you.

If in this moment you find yourself on the lazy end of the spectrum, first make sure the problem is not physical. Laziness, or a lack of energy, can come from nutrition or lack of physical condition. The first step would be to take the decision to do something about them. The next step would be to make some very short-term goals that would significantly improve how you feel. This could be working hard and planning a vacation in three months' time in order to set an incentive to get you going. Think of daily incentives that can motivate you to get out of bed and get things done.

If you find yourself at the driven end of the spectrum, remember this – you'll never get it all done, because there will always be something new to do. When you are too driven, it is easy to resent all the things you are missing out on. If you have to stay in the office each evening until very late, you may miss out on your family or social life. If you are in a relationship, look at how these habits may affect those around you. Another effect of being so driven, or even having the feeling of being pushed into achieving, is being resentful of what you are missing out on. This doesn't feel good and is often a warning sign that you are pushing yourself too hard. If you let it continue, it can lead to physical problems caused by stress.

To moderate your drive, take a mind, body and spirit approach and see how balanced you are in each of these areas. Try to put some of your drive into physical relaxation and socialization to moderate your habits.

Confusion ——————— *Clarity* ——————— *Tunnel Vision*

The common thread to these tendencies is the amount of things that you are thinking about at any one time. At the one end of the spectrum, confusion comes from trying to process too much information at one time. Like anyone that has ever had their computer screen freeze, too many requests for information at one time cause the whole thing to operate more slowly or, eventually, even break down. The same is true with the human brain.

At the other end of the spectrum, tunnel vision comes from only being able to look at one thing without considering other influences. Although we should all strive to give each thing that we do all of our attention, without questioning them and looking at alternatives it is impossible to learn new things. We all have areas in our lives that we may find confusing, and areas in which we are so steadfast in our way of thinking that we are not open to new possibilities.

If you spend a lot of time feeling confused and are unable to concentrate, always look at your physical condition first. If you have any other physical symptoms with your confusion, you may want to seek medical advice. If, however, it is not as a result of any physical problems, there are many simple ways to bring a bit more clarity. First of all, your physical surroundings, such as your home or office, can add to the confusion. If you live or work in a cluttered area, all of the objects that you can see vie for your attention. The more clutter, the more difficult it is to concentrate. Just by having a good clear out, it can lessen the distraction and make you feel more controlled. When going about your daily routine, try not to look at all the things you have to do in the day. Give 100 per cent of your focus to the one thing you need to do in the moment. You will only generate ideas by thinking about one thing at a time.

Think about what it is like to be driving through a tunnel. You are completely enclosed and unable to see anything or get communication on your radio or telephone. The same is true of tunnel vision – you are unable to see the other choices available. Gaining perspective by opening your mind to the possibility of new ideas will help you more fully to enjoy each experience you have.

Always need approval —— Confident —— Overly confident

Everyone wants to be loved and respected for the contributions they have made during their lifetime, so it is a natural thing to seek approval that what you are doing is good. Approval or non-approval is the way we learn from an early age what is right and wrong. When we get to the age that we are able to be responsible for our own decisions, the guidance that we get through other people's approval is significant. It can shape the way you feel about yourself for a long time.

Over time and with all of your life experience, you develop a knowing of what you do well, and from this comes your confidence or belief that you are able to do what you set your mind to. The more you are able to achieve even little things, the more it boosts your self-confidence. If you are on the spectrum where you constantly need approval, you have not learned to acknowledge your own successes. Why not? If you can't be proud of yourself, why should anyone else be proud of you? It all starts with you! To develop more self-confidence and less need for others' approval, you need to keep doing the things you do well and give yourself some credit for having done it. An exercise that really works a treat is simply to write down each night every little thing that you gave all of your effort to and, as a result, did well! You might have looked great when you got dressed this morning or felt really satisfied when you finished your paperwork; all minor accomplishments and, of course, the mega big ones, need to be acknowledged daily. Do it every day for six weeks and see if it makes a difference.

If you are overly confident, you can be mistaken for being arrogant, meaning that people may believe that you think you are better than they are. When you are overly confident your perspective may be jaded and you may not really be able to see the true picture. The higher you build yourself up, the further there is to fall.

Unreliable ———— *Trustworthy* ———— *Over-anxious*

These habits mainly have to do with how you view others. If you are often unreliable, it means that you often put yourself before others, or have a difficult time in understanding how best to utilize your time. Unreliability is something that happens over numerous occasions, not just occasionally.

If you are on the other end of the spectrum and dedicate your entire self to others, it means that you view a cause or other people in higher regard than your own life. This extreme position can have extreme reactions – it means that you can ignore your own welfare, or if you do it for a cause, does it justify your devotion?

If you are unreliable in some area of your life, the problem can be as simple to fix as getting more organized and connected to time. Whereas your intentions may be good in really wanting to deliver on your promise, you may often leave it until it is too late and end up letting someone down. If you do it a few times, it is easy for people to expect you to be unreliable and it is easy to live up to others' expectations. Making a list of things that you need to do on a daily basis and allocating the time you think it will take to achieve each task, will help you work towards a schedule and you are more likely to keep track of time.

Nosy —————————— *Involved* —————————— *Detached*

We are all fascinated by other people's experiences, as it often teaches us about new things. It also allows us to compare our experiences with those of others. There are many cases where, in paying too much attention to what other people do, you lose sight of what you need to do. A good example is getting involved in office politics. Although it may be interesting for a laugh, if it consumes you, you will not be paying attention to your own job. On the other side of the spectrum, if you are totally removed from everyone around you, you gain little from the experience of being in a group or social situation.

If you can't help but meddle in other people's business, you can begin to move yourself away from the situation. Rather than spending time gossiping with people, do something more constructive like going out for a walk, or talking to someone new. Another good exercise is to consciously say something nice about the person and situation to help make the gossip less harmful.

At the other extreme is detachment, meaning that you remain unattached to the situation. There are many things that can affect how you feel about letting other people become more intimate with you as a person. Sometimes detachment can be caused by not being familiar with a language or culture, and it is only by trying to become socialized that you will fit in. Other people may suffer from difficulty in letting others get to know them on a more intimate or long-term basis. If you feel that you need to become more involved with those around you, look for something nice to say and pay someone a compliment. It is an instant way to make an introduction.

The more risks you take in getting more involved with people around you, the more you will be able to talk and share some of your innermost thoughts. Always start by sharing the small things as you build your trust.

Possessive ——————— *Caring* ——————— *Inattentive*

These tendencies are about how much you pay attention to the people or things in your life. On one end of the spectrum is possessiveness, a fear that if you let something go you will no longer have it. At the other extreme is not caring enough about the things you have.

If you are possessive of people or material possessions, how do you make way for new things to enter you life? It is only by letting things go that you are able to let new things in. Being possessive and not allowing another person to have new and exciting experiences on his or her own, will make your partner very dull. It will also make them want even more independence, as they may feel stifled.

If you are inattentive towards your possessions or the people in your life, they will not last the distance. Your possessions will deteriorate and lose value and your relationships will suffer. Everyone and everything wants to be cared for. Bringing your awareness to each task you do will help you to make sure that you give things the proper attention. Simple things like making eye contact with those you come in contact with and making sure you listen to those around you will make you a more caring person.

Cautious ——————— *Considered* ——————— *Impulsive*

These habits relate to how you take action and will vary dramatically in different areas of your life. The more varied the experiences you have, the easier it may be to judge your behaviour in different situations. If you are on the cautious side in some areas of your life, it may come from deeply-held principles, or past negative experiences such as living through rationing during World War II. As a result you may be cautious just in case it might come in handy. On the other end of the spectrum is impulsive behaviour, or acting in the moment without caution. This can be great in some areas of your life, and disastrous in others if, for example, your impulsiveness gets you into financial trouble.

If you find that you are too cautious, you may not lose any ground, but you probably won't move forward either. You can often feel that life is passing you by or have feelings of regret as others seem to be having more fun. By trying new things you can change your view of the world. It is fun and exciting to have an adventurous life as you continue to refine your opinions. Remember, if you aren't in the race, you can't win.

Impulsiveness is action without thinking. If you go with your gut instinct and it has served you well in the past, and most of all it feels good, go with it whenever it feels right for you. As a general tendency, when you do things without thinking, you get into big trouble. You speak what's on your mind without looking at the situation. You spend money that you may not have or you may have a fling with someone you know nothing about. Try to moderate the impulsive behaviours that make you feel bad and have a negative effect on your life, but keep the childlike spirit within you when you feel it is right.

Don't care about – Feel your best – Overly vain appearance

In some situations we care too much about how we look to others, so we learn to judge what we are expected to appear like for certain situations. It is perfectly ok not to put on make-up or get overly dressed up if you know you are going to be in an informal situation or at home on your own. At one extreme, you never care about your appearance and don't bother to adapt to social situations and norms. At the other end of the spectrum, you care so much about what you look like, that you compare yourself to others and never feel good enough.

If you don't care about your appearance, in terms of dressing to suit others, that is fair enough. We all have a right to wear what we feel most comfortable in. It you don't care about whether your hair is combed or your clothes are clean, that is another matter. Everyone should practise good heath and hygiene habits, as they are the first things you notice. It doesn't take very much effort to make sure you are neatly presented. You can never make a first impression twice.

At the other end of the spectrum are those who model their appearance on unrealistic role models, or always want to look better. The truth is, we are all getting older, and no matter what treatment you choose to alter the effects of time, you are never going to look much younger than you are. It is great to want to look fabulous, and to do everything you want and can do to get there, but when you pay so much attention to yourself, who else is getting your affections?

Always sad ——— Working on it ——— Always happy

There may be some areas of your life which bring out strong emotional feelings. These feelings indicate whether your habits in this area are working for you or not. In areas where you are always sad, you are looking at something that you cannot have, or cannot have in a past form. If there are some (or all) areas of your life where you are happy, you have learned good habits; pay attention and cherish the thing that brings you happiness.

If you find that you are always sad, there could be physical or mental reasons behind it. It is good to discuss these feelings with your doctor. There are many therapies that can be used to treat depression or other mental illness issues. If your sadness stems from an incident that has happened in your life, there will always be a period of bereavement in which you may need to work through your emotions. Trying to think about happy rather than sad times can be a small step towards reaching the level where you actually have happier rather than sad times. Any happy thing that you can do, such as playing music or watching your favourite movie, can serve to make you feel better.

It you are always happy, bravo, you should be writing a book! It is a very good thing to find joy and happiness in every situation. I believe it is called enlightenment. Joking aside, I hope that there are many areas of your life in which you are happy. Those are the beacons that guide you on your path. If you really are happy in any area of your life, look at the elements that make it work for you. Always ask for more of the same.

So, how do your habits stack up?

I hope you find when you look at your habits overall, that your good habits far outweigh the bad ones. Trying to add more experiences into your daily routine that take advantage of your good habits will surely build your self-esteem and remove your attention from your less desirable tendencies. The rule of thumb is always to accentuate the positive to eliminate the negative. The more time spent practising your good habits and becoming more aware of your achievements; the more you will be able to find a comfortable place in the world.

The easiest way to see if your habits work for you is to reconnect, for even a few days, to everything you do. Go through your house as if you were a complete stranger. What do you see? Look at things through other people's eyes to see how others interpret your habits. Ask for input from those around you to fully understand how your habits affect them.

Everything that happens to you in your life happens for you to discriminate between what feels good and what doesn't feel good, to enable you to develop on your path to happiness. Everyone is at a different point of his or her personal path. Some people take longer than others to work through the experiences that they have had to date and decide what they really want. It is often by knowing what you don't want that you can be spurred into taking action.

It is only by looking at the degree of any problem that you can decide where on the spectrum feels comfortable for you. Either end of the spectrum is not ideal, and doesn't usually make you feel very good. Any behaviour that is excessive in one way or another probably means that you are very set in your ways and have had the habit for a long time. Working from both ends towards the middle is a peaceable way to exist.

Unfortunately, because things that are bad for you often make you feel bad, either physically – as in a smoker's cough or a hangover; or emotionally – by feeling guilty, angry or sad; or mentally – by an inability to concentrate, it is often the bad habits that inhabit a good deal of your thoughts. In addition to how they make you feel bad, you may also get negative reinforcement from those around you at work, home or socially. Some people have learned very quickly how to get what they want and achieve personal success in whatever they try. This is solely based on their ability to decipher all their experiences, run them through all levels of their consciousness to see how they feel against their moral and ethical code, and choose what feels good and will advance them. It is the active search for things that contribute to your physical, emotional, mental and spiritual well-being that enables you to change behaviours that no longer feel right for you.

Your habits have a tremendous impact on others. Your good habits serve as an example and uplift you and others, whereas your bad habits often cause friction or tension.

3.
Forgive and Forget

If I had only one piece of information to pass on to you in this entire book that I really believe can change your life, this is it. *No matter what the circumstances, no matter how much you may feel aggrieved by something someone did to you, or the circumstances of your life up to this present moment, or something that you have done in the past that you feel guilty or bad about, learning to forgive yourself and others is the only way, I repeat, the only way, that your life will move forward in a positive direction.* If I could get you to believe that you could simply write all of the hurts down on a piece of paper and set them alight and they would be gone, it would be the best thing you ever believed in. It is the simple action of wanting to feel better that enables you to summon the energy to do so.

Holding on to issues

In my Reiki healing practice, and in my work with excessive hoarders or people who have a difficult time letting go of their material possessions, I have always found there is most often a specific event that has happened in their lives that causes a feeling of dis-ease, or not feeling healthy and easy in their bodies or mind. From my study of Reiki, I was taught that something that happens on the emotional level can manifest itself on the physical level if not released. It can take between 12 and 24 months for an emotional trauma of any type, even something so small that you may not think it has impacted on you, to become a physical or mental dis-ease. In all of my work, both practising Reiki and helping people to de-junk, when I first meet a client, I ask for a history of all of their physical or emotional problems with the dates that they began. I then ask what happened to them up to two years before they started to show their symptoms. In 8 out of 10 cases, they are always able to pinpoint the traumatic event that most likely was at the root of either their physical or mental problems, or the onset of beginning to hold on to too many things.

One of my closest friends in England died several years ago, as a result of a rare liver disease. I knew her from the time I first moved to London, and over that nine-year period, she always had some sort of problem with her digestive system. She went to many different doctors to try and diagnose the problem and tried many treatments, such as replacing all the lead fillings in her teeth in case they reacted with the varied antibiotics that they used to try to treat her. When the situation became acute enough to detect it, it was already too late to do anything about it. I started to do Reiki on a weekly basis soon after she was diagnosed and was with my friend when she died. I did Reiki to work on her physical condition, as well as to work on her emotional and spiritual feelings at this stressful time in her life.

When I asked her if there were any traumatic events that had happened to her a couple of years before she started having digestive problems, I learned that she had been victimized in a bank robbery and had a sawn-off shotgun held to her head at a time when there were many other stresses in her life. I can't prove that her illness was as a result of these traumas, but I can say that it surely didn't help. She may not have thought that these traumas affected her in the way that they did. Yet two years after they began so did the onset of the illness.

I recently gave a one-day workshop on how to de-clutter your life, where there were about fifty participants who had issues with holding on to things, were unhappy with their current lifestyle and wanted to make some changes. As I started to discuss some of the more emotional issues that cause us to hold on to unpleasant memories or the material manifestations of these events, I could feel that one of the participants, an older woman in her sixties, was really holding on to something very deeply that was causing her great pain. After I finished that session, I went up to her and asked her what it was that she was unwilling to let go of. As it turned out, she was put up for adoption at birth and to this day found it impossible to forgive her mother for this action. My words of advice, and I believe them sincerely from my heart and from all of my life experience, was that the only way she could ever get over that feeling was to send love to her mother and let go of the anger and personal feelings of unworthiness that kept her stuck in the past and feeling physically unwell. A few days later I received a most heartfelt letter saying that she had really taken my advice to heart and was working on letting go and knew it was the right thing to do.

In another situation, someone whose home I helped to de-clutter held on to things that her parents would not allow her as a child, to the point that it limited access to so many areas of her home that she was forced to live in little pockets of space that would enable her to do only very basic things. She had become a serial shopper, according to her own admission, and spent a good deal of time making purchases from charity shops that didn't cost very much at the time, but over years of collecting, were worth thousands of pounds. Entire rooms were filled from floor to ceiling with plastic bags and the situation seriously impacted on her ability to socialize and live comfortably in her home.

She had grown up as the only child of older parents who were devoutly religious and very strict in her upbringing. Her father was disabled and couldn't work. Money was limited, and her mother had to look after her father, so as a child she was responsible for many household chores and often had to keep herself occupied with very little. At some point in her childhood she developed a respiratory problem and had to go to hospital. When she returned, she was more closely guarded and limited in the physical and social activities she was allowed to do. She developed a passion for music, and used the radio to comfort her and keep her company. For some reason, her mother restricted her use of the radio, and even years after her death, she was angry and rebelling against her mother for all the things she was not able to have as a child.

Who suffered as a result of her hoarding – her mother, who had passed away years ago, or my client, as a result of not being able to function in her home or in her social life? In her adult years she developed further physical problems with asthma, eczema and heart problems.

Stress, which can be caused by holding on to feelings of anger, hate or jealousy, is a leading cause of heart disease. I don't believe that it is any coincidence that you develop heart disease when you hold on to issues in your heart.

The previous chapters should have helped to bring to your awareness some beliefs, attitudes and habits that had become so routine or deeply ingrained in your personality that you may have forgotten on the conscious level that you had them. Those deeply-held beliefs, attitudes, habits or experiences generate feelings about other people and situations. How you feel about something is the first sign of how you have processed that experience. Look back at all of the beliefs and habits that you have written down and put them to the emotional test. How do they make you feel? Mark a K for Keep next to the ones that bring you good feelings and an R for Release next to the ones that make you feel bad.

Everyone can relate to the feelings of being happy, in love, content, excited, sad, frightened, angry or jealous about someone or something in their life. Positive emotions like love, happiness, contentment or excitement make you feel good on the physical, mental and emotional levels. These feelings indicate that you like or enjoy the experience and desire to have more of it or something similar. Our natural state of being is to really want to feel good, so it is always good to draw upon your vast bank of knowledge of the types of experiences that are likely to make you feel good and choose them at every chance you get.

A sense of perspective

Try making a list of which people, situations or things make you happy, give you a feeling of contentment, excitement or enthusiasm, or really motivate you. Which people, situations or things do you really love? Once you have made your list, answer the following question: if you were to teach someone one thing about what makes each of these things work for you, what would it be?

Looking at all of the things that are good and right in your life helps you to gain perspective. Even if there are some areas of your life where you seem to be stuck and unable to get what you want, there are others where things are feeling good. It is really important to look at all the good things that you have in your life and count your blessings every day. Learning to show gratitude and appreciation opens up your heart to receive the same back. The more you are able to practise and remember the feeling of good by going out and doing all the things you enjoy and make you feel happy, the better you will feel. We all have things that can uplift us, and by seeking out such people, places or situations, you can always find a way to instantly feel better.

- How much time do you generally spend each day doing things that make you happy?
- How often do you communicate with the ones you love?
- How often do you feel contented?
- How often during the day are you enthusiastic?
- How often are you motivated?
- How often do you think about all of the things that make you feel good?

Making an effort to incorporate more of these things into your life will make you feel better more of the time. You have the experiences, so use them to the maximum.

Negative emotions such as sadness, anger, jealousy, fear,

hatred or guilt certainly make you feel bad on the emotional level, and often on the physical level as well. If you hold on to these feelings and think about them and all the things that may have caused them, you go back to reliving an experience that happened in the past which you can't do anything about and doesn't feel good. This experience is also the basis for your judgement of all other experiences of a similar nature until things can get really out of proportion.

Adverse physical reactions such as high blood pressure, headaches, or other nervous-related dis-eases, often accompany the severe stress that negative emotions can have on your body. These are intended as a wake-up call to get you to take action to sort your emotions out.

Dealing with loss

If negative emotions come as a result of a shock, a tragic event or any loss in your life that is difficult to accept, these emotions are likely to surface more quickly. Anyone who has suffered a loss can easily relate to the initial jolt to your system. You may experience many emotions at the same time in the early stages of the bereavement process as your mind is trying to process all the information that you must accept. Emotions such as anger, guilt, panic, irritability or restlessness are very common, as your normal routine has been shattered. These feelings are normal reactions whenever you have a shock to the system. As it is often necessary to tell family or friends about your loss, in the initial stages you relive the experience each time you tell it. For some people this may be a cathartic experience, and if those around them are able to point out the good things about a situation, it makes it easier to handle. In the case of the death of a loved one, talking about their wonderful qualities and thinking back to the happy times you shared together can help you to find moments when you are able to feel good. The more you are able to live positive moments, the sooner it will enable you to be able to look for happy moments again.

Sometimes you may need those that you love and trust to help you understand these feelings and sometimes you may need to seek professional help. The more you are able to express these feelings and get good guidance on how to deal with them at the time, the sooner these feelings are likely to disappear. Some people may go through all the stages in a day, and others may never get over them, but it is only by working through emotions and leaving the memories of the negative experiences behind, that you are able to move forward in your life. The most important thing that you can do is to get your feelings out in the open so that you can actually deal with them, rather than keeping them locked up inside your heart and reliving them over and over again.

Dealing with regret

If the negative emotions are caused by cumulative events in a certain area of your life, such as feelings of regret or sadness, it most likely means that you keep looking back at your past decisions and wishing somehow you could change them. If you have anger and sadness it can also mean that you would like to be living in a previous time where things were better or happier, but it is not possible to have again. The more you want something that is unobtainable, the more likely you will be to experience confusion and frustration.

Dealing with guilt

When you feel guilty about something that you are not proud of, all you can do is accept responsibility, say you are sorry and move on. You can't take back the past, but you surely can learn from the experience. Looking back on the experience with the benefit of hindsight may help you to see how you could have behaved differently, but it cannot change the experience or recreate the emotions that you felt in the moment that caused you to make the decisions that you made. We all need to learn to accept our humanity – we are not perfect and do not always make the best decisions. All you can do is take the best from the experience and move on.

I recently met a lovely young woman who won a competition to have me de-clutter her home. When I arrived, I saw that her house was perfectly organized, tidy and lovely. She kept pointing out the few items that maybe had accumulated over a day or two and thought that she wasn't organized enough. She had a good job, a loving husband, a beautiful home and a young son and her life seemed to be right on track, so I couldn't understand how these minor little bits of paperwork or children's toys out of place could cause her any distress at all. She had such a kind, gentle and loving nature and obviously cared for herself and others. When I pointed out how well she had done in achieving this lovely life, she told me of her past that still haunted her.

She had two children from a previous marriage when she was very young. Her husband was loving towards the children, but abusive towards her, and when she couldn't take it any more, she ran away from the north of England to the south, wanting to start over. She felt her children would be better with her husband as he looked after them well, and left them behind. Although she has had a solid and loving relationship with her two older children which she has worked on over the last 14 years, she still carries the guilt of leaving them behind. She had just found out that her daughter was about to have a child herself at an early age and, on some level, carried the blame for her daughter's actions.

I pointed out to her that wanting something better and working hard to change her life was the best example she could ever give her children. Although running away from a problem is often not the best solution, in her case, she was very young and didn't feel that there were any options available to her, so she took a tough decision. She found a job, worked very hard, eventually met someone who she fell in love with, and went on to create a great life. To me, this sets an example that you can do anything if the desire is great enough. She never ignored her first two children and continues to have a relationship with them. The act of caring about your own self-preservation is a natural desire. Knowing that her children would be well looked after allowed her to make a choice that was right for her.

When you answer these questions, try not to think of a one-off experience, unless it is something that you have held on to over a long period of time. Try to look at the things that keep happening to you that cause these emotions.

- What things make you angry?
- What things make you sad?

- What things make you jealous?
- What things do you feel guilty about?
- What things frighten you?
- Is there anything that you hate?
- When was the last time you were angry?
- When was the last time you were sad?
- When was the last time you were jealous?
- When was the last time you felt guilty about something?
- What was the last thing that frightened you?
- When was the last time you felt hatred towards something?
- What negative emotions do you think are holding you back?

Releasing negative emotions

We have explored some of the positive emotions such as happiness, love, contentment, excitement and enthusiasm. The experiences that you are having in the present moment that bring you these emotions are those that are in your best interest and should be repeated. It's really crazy to know that sometimes we actually worry that things are going so well that something is bound to go wrong. Once you put the idea in your head, I must warn you, it is easy to find the negative if you look for it.

We have also looked at the emotions that make you feel bad as a result of an experience that you have had, such as anger, guilt or jealousy, and you would probably agree that these experiences did not make you feel good. In the present moment and in the future, you can choose not to participate in experiences that you think will make you feel bad. You are using the positive knowledge that you have gained, and your ability to differentiate, in order to avoid the experience again. If you were fired from your job for something that you had done wrong, you could learn that what you did wasn't appropriate in the situation and not do it again. You retained the positive aspects and shed the negative emotions allowing you to move forward.

If you hold on to all of the bad feelings or negative emotions that are attached to every unpleasant experience you have ever had, you will feel horrible all the time. If you held on to the anger over being fired from your job, it would really be difficult for you to go out and find another job. If you think about the pain that you may have gone through in childbirth, you may choose never to have any more children, or even worse, associate your child with the experience of pain. If you hold on to the deep sadness of losing a loved one, you may never be able to experience a new love, as you cannot open your heart enough to release the pain and allow more love in. At some time you must let go of negative emotions if you truly want to feel better.

Some people can release negative feelings, and be completely rid of them. You get angry that you stub your toe on a piece of furniture and may even act out towards the furniture by yelling at it or hitting it. Once the physical pain subsides, you forget about it in probably a matter of minutes. Or you have a fight with your partner over something important to you in the moment, and get angry and stay angry for some time, not feeling very good in the process. A good healthy argument can help clear the air as long as you play by the rules. Don't dredge up things from the past and look towards coming to an amicable resolution before ending your conversation.

If, however, you have had a more shocking experience that

brings about negative feelings, like an unexpected death or getting made redundant from work, there is a deeper sense of feeling let down by some force outside your control, and this can take longer to work through. The truth is, you won't feel better physically, mentally, emotionally or spiritually until you are able to take the leap from dwelling on the negative aspects of the event. Isn't today a good day to start to feel better?

They say that time is a healer, and in many cases this is true. Something unexpected may happen at some time in the future to enable you to let go of a negative experience and move on. Your memories may fade and with them some of the emotions of the experience, although for all the time that you held on to the negative feelings, you were not living a joyful existence. By waiting for something better to *happen*, you take the control away from yourself and leave it to fate. If you were given the choice to feel good by doing and experiencing things that make you feel good, or to feel bad by doing and experiencing things that make you feel bad, you will probably say that you would always choose to have the good feeling or experience. If this is the case, why do we often choose to continue feeling bad? Does feeling bad ever change the circumstances?

In the next chapter, we will work on releasing all the experiences that you list below, along with all of the beliefs, habits and attitudes you have already determined you are ready to release by placing an R next to them.

- List all of the negative experiences you have had in the past that still cause you to feel bad. Don't go into any detail about the experience, just a short description will do.
- List any experiences that have happened to those you

know or more generally in your town, country or the
world, that cause you to have negative emotions.
- Write down when the event happened, or when you
started to feel negative about the things that are
outside your personal experience.
- Next to the event and the date, write down the
emotions that you associate with the event – such as
anger or hatred. Don't make any judgements about
the answers.
- On a scale of one being the easiest and ten the
hardest, go through each event and order them by
how easy you think it would be for you to let go of
the negative feelings. For example, if you have 10
experiences, the one that you think is the easiest is
1 and the next easiest is 2.
- Take a look at the beliefs and habits that you have
marked with an R to release and go through the
same process of numbering in order of the easiest
you think you will be able to release.

There are many methods to help you to release thoughts,
attitudes, habits, negative feelings and experiences from your
conscious as well as your subconscious levels, which will
enable you to forgive yourself and others for events in your
life. Some methods may work better than other methods
because of the degree of negative feelings attached to the
experience and the way you process information. Different
methods are also good for releasing different types of feelings,
so you may want to try a combination for the different issues
you want to resolve. I have used all of these methods successfully to help people let go of things from the past that no
longer serve a useful function in their lives.

Wearing my Reiki hat, I believe that once you remove a

vibration from your physical being, it helps to bring everything back to a natural and harmonious state of being. Just like removing a piece of furniture (which is made of the vibrations of the molecules that comprise the object) from a room, once the furniture is gone, as long as you choose to leave it out of the room, it will be gone forever. Therefore, your ability to release negative emotions that hold you back from being happy and joyous can disappear forever if you make that conscious choice to do so.

Intention

In order for any of the methods to work, however, you must have intention. This means that you have made a clear and firm decision about what you want. In the case of wanting to release negative feelings, you have to actively want to feel better. Without the desire to feel well and truly better, you will never get there.

It is often easier to focus on feeling bad, as there is usually a physical symptom associated with it that can easily consume your attention. It is always good to have an incentive to keep your attention focused. If you have negative feelings about your body weight and you are trying to release them, holding a realistic vision of where you want to be in a month's time, three months' time and a year from now acts as a great incentive. The more enthusiastic you get about the end result, the more quickly you will be able to release the old feelings.

Sometimes you may not be able to release things in one go, but rather you may need to take small steps on a daily basis to get where you want to be. Knowing how you want to feel and reaching for things that help you feel that way is a great way to take control of your own well-being. Just as in infancy and childhood when you drink milk to build strong bones cumulatively over time, the little bit better that you can feel on a daily basis also has cumulative effects over time. The stronger and happier you feel, the better choices and decisions you will make.

Always start with the easiest thing on your list. Something that you already feel ready to release will be easier to let go of, and by the time you get to the end of the list, you will be an old pro. As you start to release these emotions you will feel lighter and more alive and connected with what is going on around you. Your judgement will feel better and you will gain self-confidence. You will feel more attractive in yourself and more confident in your place in the world. One small step every day will start the next day feeling even better and more confident and you will do it all by making the choice, right now, that you want to feel better. And every day you will continue to make choices that make you feel good. When you are so focused on the good and positive there is very little time for the negative to creep in. You must stay connected to the present moment to see the change happen. Dipping back into the past can quickly set you back.

As a matter of practice

Remove your attention from the negative feeling or situation, even if it is only for a few minutes more each day

This probably sounds like I am telling you to stick your head in the sand and ignore a situation that is bothering you, when in fact it is the complete reverse. Dwelling on our negative thoughts or emotions means that we are always looking at or thinking about something that makes us feel bad. The more you look for something bad, the more easily you will find it in every aspect of your life. If you look at the bad aspects of taking public transportation, every day you do it, you will feel bad. If you concentrate on a positive action instead, like reading a paper or looking at everyone on the train or bus and seeing what is interesting about them, you will feel better. It may not make public transportation high on your list of things you would choose, but if you have to do it, choose to feel better in the process.

Here is how it works with an emotion like jealousy. To be jealous, you are comparing yourself with others, and wanting something that they have and you don't have. You are focusing on what you do not have and this always feels bad. The more you continue to look at the things that make you jealous, the worse you feel. In order to have this feeling, you have to be continually looking at or talking about what others have. What feels better, longing for a swim in your neighbour's pool, or thinking about ways that you could manage to have a place with a pool in the future? Positive action and thoughts always feel like the best choice. To release the feeling of jealousy, simply don't look at what it is that makes you jealous and focus more on what you want, rather than what you don't have. There is an enormous difference in the way it makes you feel!

We all have small annoyances every day that can really work our nerves. My pet hate is trying to get a real live person to talk to me on the end of the phone, rather than the endless loop of mechanized choices that you make that take time and never seem to solve your problem. For months, as I had to sort out a computer problem, I had a phone tucked in my shoulder as I waited, and continued to get angrier and angrier each time I phoned. In addition to the anger, I developed really bad muscle tension in my shoulder and neither of the symptoms made me feel very good. The pain in my shoulder, because it really hurt, brought my awareness to the situation and I realized that I needed to act to sort it out. Looking for a positive solution, I decided to get a speakerphone that would at least alleviate the pain in my shoulder, and indeed it did the trick. Because feeling physically better lifted me up, I realized that with the speakerphone I could continue to work while I was on endless hold, so I felt much better about not wasting my time. Rather than focusing on how angry I was with the situation with my computer, I was able to take constructive action and eventually get it sorted out. I still don't like those phone systems, but I don't make myself suffer in the process any longer.

With emotions such as deep sadness from a loss, each day you have to think a bit more about what you gained from the experience or choose to partake of an activity that will take your mind away from the situation altogether. Thinking about all of the things that you have gained forever as a result of having that person in your life is a positive way to turn mourning into celebration. I think about all of my family and friends who have passed on or live in different countries every day and always feel their positive influences around me, because they are a part of who I am. If it is still painful and hurts too much, whenever you begin to feel sadness coming on, do a small thing that will take your mind away from it. Anything that will make you feel even a bit more positive for five minutes will be less time spent on feeling bad.

- Do you think that you have any negative situations that would benefit from thinking about them less?
- Are there any places that you go to that make you feel bad?
- Do you have anything in your house that makes you feel bad?

Get rid of the physical reminders of the negative feelings or experiences that make you feel bad

De-junk your material possessions so that you have less reminders of the negative experience. Your senses enhance each experience you have. If you are watching the news about a war on television, you may be likely to remember it, because you saw it and it evoked an emotion. If you hear music that you associate with a negative experience, it can bring back the feelings of the negative experience because the music made the experience memorable. We often keep lots of memorable reminders in the form of clothing, music, art, photographs, and everything else imaginable, to remind us about the experiences we have had. If you hold on to material possessions that remind you of something that makes you feel bad, you have the choice to remove it to feel better. By choosing what material possessions you surround yourself with, you can release many things that do not make you feel good or keep you stuck in the past. Why torture yourself when it doesn't feel very good and surely doesn't add anything that you want to your life experience?

It is easy to hold on to things because you don't want to hurt someone else's feelings. You can relate to holding on to a gift that you receive and don't like but are afraid that the person will notice that you don't have it. Over the years, all these things add up. With the exorbitant cost of housing, space is at a premium, so why take up limited space with things you don't like? Acknowledge to yourself that the gift was given with love, which is the positive experience you gain, and let the article go on to someone who will appreciate it better. Selling your possessions can generate some money to do something or get something you like better. If money is not the motivation, open up your heart and give it away.

Friends, family or your local charity shops will be grateful and you will feel good inside.

The feeling of guilt and sadness can be greater in situations where any type of loss is involved. Often material possessions are all that is left to remind you of a person and it can take time to let many of them go, as there is a feeling of disloyalty to the memory of the person who has gone. In death, others can benefit from your loss and often there is a feeling of comfort in knowing that.

For example, a young girl in her early twenties inherited a beautiful Queen Anne home in the northern part of England. Although lovely on the outside, the house was in a terrible state of repair on the inside, as the owner bred dogs and was in failing health prior to her death. The woman was quite a fascinating character and was an avid collector of many interesting and valuable artworks and collectibles, many of which were starting to deteriorate and lose their value as a result of the condition of the house. She had died at home and was not found until some time later, making the situation inside the home even more desperate.

The young girl was studying and living in London at the time and had a boyfriend there. The inheritance came out of the blue. The woman was not a close relative, but a very close friend of the family that she had spent some time with as a child and young adult and had not spoken to or seen for a while. She had been given an amazing gift, but it meant a complete change of lifestyle that had many personal and professional ramifications. She chose to move there, continue her studies there and have a long-distance relationship while she tried to sort out the house.

The kitchen was the first priority as the local authorities had condemned it. She cleaned everything up and painted a room for herself in this enormous house, then left all the other rooms as they had been. It felt as if the woman were still in the house. Because this woman's life's work was in the home, the young girl's parents encouraged her to keep things, making it difficult for her to stamp her own personality on the home. She felt enormous guilt at selling off or giving away someone else's life's work, but she really needed to in order to continue to improve both the physical structure and atmosphere of her new home. When she finally took the decision to clear it out and sell or give things on, she had a very mature approach for her age. She kept the things that had meaning or sentiment to her personally and took the responsibility to forward the research to an organization that would benefit from it. She raised tens of thousands of pounds in the process and was able to use the funds to lovingly restore the home and claim it as her own.

- Are you holding on to gifts you don't like? List and dispose.
- Are there any objects that you find it painful to look at? If so, list them and look at ways to best pass them on.
- Are you holding on to memories from relationships that have ended? If so, why?
- Are you holding on to things because you are afraid you won't have enough if you let them go?

Physical exercise can help you release built up negative energy

A good fitness routine can help you feel better in your physical body and give you the added strength to help you get over the negative emotions or experiences you want to release. The stronger and better you feel on the outside, the more energy you have to tackle the tougher issues.

Prolonged continuous exercise such as running, cycling or long-distance swimming helps to contribute to the production of endorphins, a natural, morphine-like substance that is released by the brain and produces what you have probably heard of as a 'runner's high' or the second wind that you get after you have worked out for a prolonged period of time. Endorphins help to block out pain and promote a feeling of well-being and euphoria. Some research suggests that endorphins enhance the immune system, relieve pain, reduce stress and delay the ageing process. What they certainly do, is make you feel better.

A wide range of activities produces endorphins. They are the hormones produced during natural childbirth that allow both the mother and child a 'high' during the birthing process, regardless of the pain involved. Having sex also releases endorphins that can account for the feelings you may have during and after sex. Other activities that release endorphins are a prolonged fit of laughter, eating certain spicy foods and complementary therapies such as acupuncture or osteopathy.

Creative visualizations can help creative thinkers to let things go

Creative thinkers use the right side of the brain which is more intuitive, creative, and able to look at things as a whole.

Creative personalities may be more random and holistic and focused on aesthetics and may be able to see things that they remember in great detail. There is a great success rate in releasing emotional experiences in creative thinkers who visually imagine that they are releasing them. If you fit into this category, have a look at the experiences that you are ready to release, starting with the easiest first, and try this release visualization.

Make sure before you start that you are wearing comfortable clothing and sitting in a comfortable chair with your back against the back of the chair and feet on the ground. You can do this exercise lying in bed, but may become so relaxed you fall asleep! Always start by closing your eyes and taking a deep breath in to the count of 5, and out to the count of 5, making sure you are keeping your shoulders level. Do this 3 times.

To release an emotion:
Imagine that you are in your favourite outdoor space and it is a perfect day. The sun is shining and you are dressed comfortably and you decide to find a place to sit. You take in everything around you and the warmth of the sun is making you feel very relaxed. You decide to close your eyes and have a little rest, and as you begin to relax, you think about a feeling that you are ready to release and about where that feeling is on your body. As you bring your awareness to the part of your body in which you feel that emotion, you feel an overwhelming sense of love and happiness overtaking you. You feel a rush and flow of energy that is warm or tingling that starts at the very top of your head and is

sending love to all the thoughts that you may have in your mind. It continues down to your heart and it stays there for a while, spreading golden, healing rays to release all negative feelings. The energy continues to flow to the part of your body that is feeling an emotion that is ready to be released and as it gets there, you immediately feel that the emotion has been released as you allow the love in your heart to let it go.

To release an experience:
Imagine that you are in a lovely room, sitting at a desk by the window. The sun is streaming in through the window and it is open a crack so you can hear the laughter of children playing in the background. You bring your awareness back to the desk and you realize that you are about to write a letter to someone. In this letter you want to tell someone that you forgive him or her for something they have done. As you start to write this letter, you feel lighter, with a sense of warmth around your heart and gentle breezes flowing around you. You start to pour out all of your sentiments and you feel a tremendous sense of release as you finish your letter. You know that the recipient, wherever they may be, receives it and feels the love flow from your heart and sends it back.

You slowly bring your awareness to the sounds that you can hear out the window and the sun on your face. You start to wiggle your toes and gently feel yourself back in your comfortable chair. In your own time open your eyes and see how much lighter you really do feel.

Writing things down can help logical thinkers to let things go

Left-brain thinkers are logical and rational, and have a tendency to look at parts rather than the whole. A left-brain personality wants to be accurate, analytical and, most of all, wants to understand the situation. In order to release emotions or experiences, there often has to be a good reason to do it. Writing down all the positive benefits of letting go of the experience or emotion will often help a left-brained person to gain control of the situation.

> Start in the same comfortable position, in a place you can also write things down. Take a few deep breaths in to the count of five and out to the count of five and focus on your breath as you inhale deeply and exhale deeply. When you are feeling relaxed and ready, take a look at your list and choose the easiest emotions or experiences that you feel ready to release. Make a list of 25 reasons why letting go of the experience will improve your life. Try to write down another 25 reasons and keep going until you can't think of any more. Your logical brain can analyse the information and help you to see that holding on to the negative feelings is not in your best interest.

Personal rituals are a ceremonial way to release things and to ask for help from a more spiritual place

All cultures have ceremonial practices to usher in life, reach the age of maturity, celebrate marriage and death, and many other occasions. Asking a force higher than yourself for the wisdom and courage to move on in your life is a powerful way of getting the help that you need. When you release things into the universe for divine help and guidance and have faith that the universe is there to help, it can uplift you in many ways. Developing your own personal rituals on a routine basis can help you to stay connected to your more spiritual side.

Many people take solace in their faith when they have negative experiences. You may speak with a religious leader, or meditate in a sacred place, or simply say your prayers on a regular basis. In forming your prayers, always first ask that your thoughts are for the highest good of all involved and invite your guides and angels to participate in the process. If you are able to open your mind to the possibilities that may exist, you will be surprised by the outcome.

I have a wonderfully spiritual friend and student who always performs a ritual to celebrate the full moon. The moon is the ruler of your emotions, so the full moon is always a great time to release your negative emotions. Each month, she writes a thank-you letter to the universe for all the goodness in her life. She writes down some of her goals and desires and asks that she may have help to receive them. She goes to her lovely garden, lights a candle, says her prayers of thanks and sets her letter alight to go off to the universe. It certainly has worked for her. In the last year she married, started her own successful business, purchased a new home and is one of the happiest and most delightful people I know.

If you feel that you are able to write down the negative things that you are ready to release and send them off to the universe, try a ritual of your own. Begin by writing down all of the negative emotions that you are ready to release, and ask that they be transmuted into positive and loving energy. Find a peaceful space where you can commune with nature and ask for the help you need to release these negative thoughts. Make sure you are in a safe place to burn your letter and as you set it alight and see the ashes rise, know that your prayers have been heard. Unless you try it, you will never know if it can work for you!

To release negative energies in your home, try burning a sage stick. A ritual known as smudging and used by Native American Indians, it is said to purify both sickness and bad feelings and it has always worked to raise the energy in homes that I visit. According to legend, start in the easternmost part of the room, walking slowly around the perimeter of the room and letting the smoke waft into each corner, a place where negative energy can collect. To put out the sage stick when you are finished, dip it in a pot of sand or earth.

Dried sage sticks are available in many new age shops or on the Internet.

Complementary therapies can help release blockages of energy to enable you to release unwanted thoughts and experiences

Complementary therapies can also help you to feel better on the physical level. As holistic healing is more readily acceptable and available to mainstream society, it is very easy to experiment and find one that works for you. As a Reiki practitioner on the personal and professional level, I can honestly say that

I have seen many miraculous results. This gentle energy works effortlessly to release stubborn blockages in the mental, physical and emotional levels. There are many other forms of complementary therapies that I have tried and I do believe that they can all work when, and only when, you are ready to let things go. At the end of the book I include a list of national organizations that you can explore to find out more information about the ones that you think might work for you.

Never be afraid to seek professional help to solve a problem

It is easy to become embarrassed or ashamed that you are not able to work some things out on your own. Often, a more objective third party can be easier to talk to than someone who may be familiar with your circumstances. The ultimate goal is to feel good and you should try any positive method that can help you achieve that goal. If you have some deep issues that you don't seem able to release, try to find a professional counsellor who you can develop a rapport with to gain perspective on the issues you are trying to release.

4.

Positive Mental Attitude

I am hopeful that in the first two chapters you were able to identify some attitudes and habits that have been cluttering up your mind and preventing you from being fully happy and relaxed in your life. In Chapter 3, there are many methods to help you start the de-junking process. Some deeply-held attitudes and habits may take a bit of time to work through, but each small step forward that you take enables you to lighten the load and feel stronger in the process.

One of the easiest ways to prevent mental clutter is by learning to develop a positive mental attitude. Once you are able to develop the habit of looking at the best that each experience has to offer, you will filter out the negative influences around you. A positive mental attitude is a can-do attitude which helps you find solutions to even the biggest problems. When you have a positive attitude, you will have more fun and also find that you attract people who are positive and energetic.

If you look around you at the successful people you know or read about, you will find that they come from a wide variety of backgrounds. The common thread that unites them is a positive mental attitude (PMA). Successful people look at the desired outcome rather than at the obstacles they may encounter along the way. If one thing doesn't work, they learn from the experience and keep looking for new ways to get what they want. From conflict new ideas are born.

Successful people are prepared to take risks and try new

things. Their eagerness and enthusiasm help them achieve their desired goals, as the truth is that most people like to back a winner! Wouldn't you prefer to be around someone who feels confident and gives you energy rather than someone who is lacking in confidence and brings your energy down?

We all go through rough patches in life, and it is easy to believe, when you're down, that you are always going to feel like that. You start to think about all your problems and you go further down until it becomes difficult to remove your thoughts from all the negative things in your life. I've been there and I know many people who spend more time worrying about things than taking part in life. It doesn't feel good, and no matter how bad your circumstances may be, a positive attitude is the only way you will feel better and get on with your life.

Throughout this chapter there are many strategies to help you develop a more positive outlook about your life that can impact on your health, financial stability and overall happiness. By getting into a positive frame of mind, you will keep all the mental clutter that brings you down from creeping back into your life.

So what does a PMA get you?

First and foremost, with a PMA you are going to feel immediately better in every situation you face. Physically better, emotionally better and mentally better; you will start to receive the benefits the minute you begin to practise it and for as long as you continue to practise it. It will always work, because feeling positive can never make you feel bad, and it really is as simple as that. The effects of a PMA are cumulative – the more you practise, the more areas of your life will improve.

I have a very close friend, who is also a Reiki healer, who really hates the dentist: so much so, that the sound of the drill in a waiting room can cause her to bolt. She needed to have some complicated work done on her teeth, and knew that it was really important to get the work done. She decided that she would try a more positive approach and practise Reiki while she was letting the dentist do his work. It is illegal to practise Reiki on teeth in the UK, but she was sending healing energy to the situation, while the dentist was doing the work. She imagined purple healing energy around her mouth and continued to focus on the healing until the procedure was complete. The dentist said he had never thanked anyone before for being such an open patient and allowing him to do what he had to do. She now knows that her positive energy made her feel better in the dentist's chair and also allowed the dentist to more easily do something that would benefit her. The positive outlook allowed an easy solution! I know that she will never worry about going to the dentist again.

How can you develop a PMA?

Everything that we do springs from our desire, so to develop a PMA, you have to want to feel better than you are feeling now, in one or more areas of your life. The first step is to take complete responsibility from this minute forward for every choice you make. Don't worry because the choices don't always have to be big choices in order to make you feel better. The last step is to always take the choice that is for your highest good; in other words, it moves you in the direction of what you want. It can be what you want in the minute, next week or in ten years' time; the timescale does not matter.

You can choose whether you spend time looking your best before you face the day, or whether you rush out of bed and throw yourself together in a dishevelled heap. One choice may help you advance your career, or self-image; the other surely won't. You can choose whether commuting to work is your biggest nightmare, or use the time to do something on the train or bus that makes you relax or get prepared for the day. One choice will make you feel miserable; the other will feel better. And even if you are at your lowest point, living on the streets with no sense of hope, if you choose to seek a solution to your problem and really want to have a better life, you can take one small step to improve your condition and make yourself feel better. Without exception! Taking positive action increases your chances of success and the enjoyment of your life by 100 per cent.

What if you don't know what you want?

I want to tell you a personal story about a time in my life, after graduating from university, when I was at my absolute lowest point.

> Although I got very good grades in school, I never had a clear-cut idea of what I wanted to do with my life. I was encouraged to go to university, even though I was the only one in my family to do so. In those days, when looking for a practical career, as a woman you were guided towards nursing or education. I chose the latter, and although I really enjoyed teaching, I found that I

really hated doing it in schools. I was faced with really not knowing at all what I wanted to do with my life, and also feeling guilty that I had spent four years studying something I didn't want to do. It wasn't just the career that was worrying me. I was in a relationship that wasn't working, and I didn't even know where I wanted to live. I was constantly confused and feeling in a daze, as there were so many possibilities and I had no idea what to do. I was so consumed by having to make such big decisions that I couldn't make even the smallest decision, and I really thought that I was having a nervous breakdown. This state of confusion lasted for about a year.

I wish I could tell you the one thing that happened to me that made me shift my attention, but it was almost as quick as that. It seemed as if a veil had been lifted and I realized that I did not have to make the decision about what I wanted for the rest of my life. All I had to think about was what I wanted to do in the moment to make myself feel better. I moved in with friends, took a job in a retail store and made the money to pay the rent and to pay back my loans from university.

Even though I knew the job wasn't what I really wanted to do, I gave it my best efforts. I soon headed up one department and then several departments, and in the process met a customer who offered me another job; this time in politics. It meant that I had to move to another state – from Vermont, where I was living at the time, to Virginia. That campaign led to another campaign and I kept meeting people who gave me opportunities to try things that I had never done before. I went from politics to property and led a lifestyle that just years before I could not have imagined. I always went with my gut instinct and always, always, took a risk if it felt like the right thing to do. I travelled to most parts of America, met presidents and movie stars, and every step of the way gained more and more confidence to realize that if you believe you can do something, you can find a way to do it.

The point is you don't have to know what you want when you grow up, because you are always growing and always changing what you want. Worrying about the big stuff doesn't feel very good because where you want to be in the future can be so far away from where you are that if you think about how hard, or how long, it might take to get there, you could easily stop trying because it doesn't feel achievable. What is achievable is doing something positive in the moment to feel like you are taking a step in the right direction.

Where do you begin?

You have already begun the process by identifying attitudes, beliefs and habits that no longer serve you well, and making a list of all the things that make you feel good about yourself. If I were you, I would take the list of those things that no longer work, and ceremonially burn it as a metaphoric release of these vibrations from your body. I would then put the positive list where I could see it every day. You can only develop self-esteem if you begin to look at all of your wonderful characteristics and traits, and work positively to develop them further because they make you feel good.

We are going to look at the effects of a PMA in the areas of your health, wealth and happiness. A good place to start is with your physical body for three reasons:

- Without it, the game is up
- If you have any physical discomfort, it is easy to focus on the pain
- Your physical body, in the form of your appearance, is what you say about yourself to the world.

Immediate ways for you to feel better:

No matter what type of dis-ease you have, you have to WANT to be better

If you give up the will to live, or spend a lot of time focusing on a less serious illness, not only do you feel bad in the moment, but it can also prevent you from taking active measures to feel better. There are many pain reduction techniques that we will discuss at the end of this chapter that can help you take your mind away from the pain to help you feel better in the moment, and gain a more optimistic perspective. It is by actively wanting your body to return to a natural state of harmony, and by doing everything you can to achieve it, that you have the PMA to help the healing process along. I have witnessed quite a few miracles of the power of the mind to make me an everlasting believer.

Another friend of mine suffered from HIV and was desperately ill. He was at the hospital across the street from my house and I asked if he would like to have some Reiki, as he had come for a session a few times before. I checked with the doctors who had no objections, and I began popping in once a day to do some work with Reiki and some crystal healing.

One of his biggest concerns was that he had not

made a last will and testament and this weighed heavily on his mind. With the concerted efforts of quite a few good people, we gathered around and took down the last wishes that he was clearly able to state. Completing something that he wanted to do seemed to bring him great comfort.

I missed a day of Reiki and went to the hospital on the following day to see how he was doing. I was amazed to find him up and walking around and doing so much better. He made a recovery and got out of the hospital but was told that in order to live, he required a new liver within the next six months. He was HIV positive, in his mid-fifties and, at this time, the long-term odds did not seem to be in his favour. I continued to see him and felt that if he really wanted to live, it wasn't yet his time to go.

Three months later, as time was passing quickly, he picked up the crystal that I had given him, put it on his stomach, and said out loud that he wanted a new liver. The next day he got a 6 a.m. call telling him to be at the hospital immediately and, believe it or not, he had a liver transplant that morning and was alert enough to call me in the afternoon to tell me what had happened. It is over a year on and he has gained weight, is able to travel and doing amazingly well.

My shining example is even closer to my heart. My 94-year-old mother is in great mental health and, as you would expect from someone of that age, shows some signs of physical ageing on the body, as well as some respiratory problems that are under control. Over time she has developed osteoporosis, which limits her ability to get around without the aid of a walking stick.

It was recently found that she had high levels of calcium in her blood, meaning that the calcium in her bones was, in effect, leaching off, causing her bones to weaken. After meeting with a specialist, she was diagnosed with an abnormal parathyroid gland, which causes a hormone to be released into the body, robbing calcium from the bones. It was not a life-threatening illness, but a potentially debilitating one, and required a minor surgical procedure to remove the gland.

On the positive side, regardless of your age, you are able to strengthen your bones by the amount of calcium you have in your diet and dietary supplements. (Vitamin D is necessary to help your body absorb calcium. The primary source of Vitamin D is the sun.) My mother was able to absorb calcium, but the malfunctioning gland robbed it, so if the gland were removed, her bones could strengthen. On the negative side, having any surgery at that age is a frightening prospect. My two older sisters were initially against it, but my mother was adamant that she did not want to be bedridden and wanted to have the procedure done. I flew back to the States to be with my mother and sisters during this time. The operation was less than an hour in length and my mum came through it with flying colours. She was out of the recovery room in 1½ hours and the first thing she asked for was her make-up. If that doesn't show clear signs of wanting to feel the best you can in the circumstances, I can't think of any better example. She was home 24 hours after that and resumed her daily routine of getting up early, tending to her personal needs and then to her daily household routine. She never complained about pain, or tiredness; she just got on with it and did the things that made her feel better.

Whatever your destiny may be, looking for all the things that make you feel good and taking active steps to feel better will help to make you feel good for all the days you have.

Get regular check-ups

The big thing that gets in the way of most people getting regular medical check-ups is often the fear of what they might find. Fear makes you feel awful, both physically and mentally. By focusing your energy on all of the negative things that a doctor may find, you live a negative experience by your own choice. Those with a PMA go to the doctor for their routine check-ups for confirmation that all is well. If anything is detected, it is often at an early enough stage that it can be treated successfully. It is only by loving your body and wanting to keep it in its best operating condition that you make the best choices to help you maintain a healthy and fit body. Start today by making an appointment to visit your doctor or dentist for any overdue check-ups. To overcome the fear when you get there, remove your thoughts from the worry and occupy them with something else. Try the following:

- Bring a portable music player and listen to something that uplifts you.
- Escape in a book or something that holds your attention.
- Try the 'Perfect Getaway' meditation at the end of the chapter.
- Bring along a friend to keep you company.
- Ask your doctor to tell you the date the results are due so you don't worry needlessly for longer than necessary.

Eat better to feel better

Your food is like the fuel that you put into your car to make it run. Good quality gas makes an engine run smoothly, as putting good quality food into your body helps it to run smoothly for longer. Just as putting sugar in an engine makes it seize, the effect of eating too much sugar on the physical body is damaging and is one of the leading causes of obesity. Your food intake is the easiest way for you to regulate the amount of mental and physical energy you have in your body.

In most situations, you have complete control over what you choose to eat in order to make you feel at your best. Paying attention to eating the foods that are right for you, at the times when your body requires energy to work efficiently and make you feel your best, is a positive way to make yourself feel better in the moment. It is also a positive step to help you achieve your ideal body weight for your age and height over a longer-term period of time. In as little as six weeks of actively pursuing healthy and delicious options in your food choices, you can really begin to see a difference in your physical appearance as well as how much more energy you have when you need it.

Fresh foods are better than prepared foods as they have fewer negative additives. To increase your knowledge of the foods you eat, always look at the packaging. The ingredients are always listed in order of the largest first, so if the foods you are eating have high quantities of sugar or fat at the top of the list, you know that they are high in things you don't want to eat. Looking for fresh substitutes is an easy way to cut down on unwanted calories. Something as simple as substituting fresh strawberries for strawberry jam, or a natural fruit juice with no additives for a high-sugar fizzy drink can cut out unwanted calories and make you feel better in the process.

To develop a PMA about food, rather than looking at all of the things that you can't have, as if often the case when you choose to diet, focus your energy on all the foods you can eat. As is always the case, looking at what you don't have, or can't have, makes you feel bad, and looking at all of the things you can have makes you feel better.

Physical exercise helps the body and the mind

All muscles in the body need a good daily workout to stay toned. In the short term, if you participate in prolonged exercise you may feel good as a result of the endorphins that are released by the brain. In the long term, physical exercise will help you to feel and look younger, for as long as you continue to participate. You may gain self-confidence by setting goals and targets that are within your reach to enable you to practise winning – even if you are betting against yourself. Watch any successful athlete when they are participating in their sport and you will be able to see the enormous focus of energy that it takes to challenge your body in that way.

To develop a PMA about physical fitness, start by shifting your attitude about the physical routines you already do on a daily basis. By doing them with purpose rather than out of need, you can gain added physical benefits. If walking is part of your daily routine, walk with purpose. Pick up your pace a bit and make it enjoyable by taking in the sights and sounds around you. Opt for the stairs rather than the lift for a cardio workout. If housework is part of your daily or weekly routine, do it with purpose. Turn on the music, get in the mood and lose calories and inches as you vacuum up the dirt in the process. Playing with your kids, gardening or even cleaning your car are positive ways to get fit and accomplish something in the process.

Your brain is also a muscle that needs exercise to stay on top form. It is sad to see the effects of a lack of mental stimulation on the mind, body and spirit, as can be the case with the elderly population. Actively using your brain to challenge it and learn something new is another PMA that will help your body serve you well over time. Reading, studying and sharing your views and opinions with others can help keep your mind stimulated and on a positive track.

First impressions count

How you present yourself to the world speaks volumes about how you feel about yourself. If you want a job, a relationship, or people to take you seriously, you must first take care of yourself and look the part. No matter how you view your physical characteristics, or worry about the clothing in your wardrobe, it is always easy to be neat and clean. To develop a PMA about your appearance, you have to take the time and effort to look in the mirror and like what you see.

Personal hygiene is the most important part of your appearance and, as such, you should give adequate time to the process. Rather than rushing out of the house just in time, to make sure you feel and look your best, allow 30 minutes at the minimum to take care of your personal needs such as bathing, shaving, deodorizing, and looking after your hair and make-up if appropriate. It is one of the most important things that you can do to get your day off to the best start possible, and will have a dramatic impact on how others view you and, often, but maybe not fairly, your abilities.

Regardless of your economic circumstances, you can always look your best. To achieve this, always keep your clothing clean and ironed. It doesn't cost much and has a huge impact on your appearance. Use your past experiences of similar situations to determine the appropriate dress for the occasion. In that for most weddings you wouldn't wear jeans, you probably wouldn't wear very formal clothes into the office. Stick to light scents for the daytime if you are around other people and be sensitive to the amount that you put on. A little goes a long way.

There are many small things that you can do for a quick appearance fix. A haircut or change of hair colour can instantly make you feel like a new person. Assess your wardrobe for the clothing that makes you feel good and confident and look for more of the same. Assembling a capsule wardrobe for specific occasions can help take the terror out of what to wear. If you are in doubt, always look for a mentor, or a friend whose style you admire. It is positive to have a positive role model to look up to.

Let's move on to the area of wealth

This is an area that most people spend a good part of their life worrying about, and not enough time enjoying. From all that I have seen, people who have money can worry about it just as much as people who do not. Either worrying about losing what you have, or not having enough, definitely makes you feel bad and doesn't get you what you want. Most certainly, it doesn't enable you to enjoy what you do have in the current moment.

- Your attitude to money will influence how much you have.
- Anyone can increase his or her personal wealth by wanting more.

Assess your current situation

To develop a PMA in the area of your financial wealth, begin by looking at where you are in the current moment. Just as a company will look at its assets and liabilities on a frequent basis to see if they are profitable and moving in the right direction, you need to take control of your personal financial position. The easiest way to do this is to develop a good practice of dealing with bills and paperwork. In all the de-cluttering work I do, unopened and saved paperwork is one of the biggest culprits. If you don't look after your affairs, who else will? If your affairs are in good order, it shouldn't take more than a few hours to add up the sums, but can take several days if it is something you have avoided in the past. Set aside enough uninterrupted time to get the job done, and don't make it seem like a chore. Put on some music that puts you in a good frame of mind, and look at it as the first step towards having more abundance in your life.

- Open all post and immediately throw out, recycle or shred anything that is outdated or junk.
- Check bank statements and credit card statements as soon as they arrive to make sure that all is in order. By paying attention to your monthly balances, it helps you to budget and plan for future purchases.
- Make a list of your major assets, such as home, car, savings, or any other investment.
- Make a list of all the income you receive.
- Make a list of your regular monthly outgoings, such as rent, mortgage, utilities, transportation, insurance, food and any other monthly expenses.
- Make a list of all outstanding balances.

- Subtract the regular monthly expenses from your income.
- Look at how much you have left over to pay off outstanding balances.
- Make a list of anything that requires urgent attention.

Always deal with the most urgent problems first, as they cause stress and make you feel bad. If you are in debt, this is a leading factor in stress and can eventually lead to physical and emotional dis-ease. The best way to tackle debt is to talk about it with your bank or creditors and work out a plan to pay off what you owe. Once you take positive action, you have honoured a commitment and will find it easier to solve the problem. Even if you pay off a small amount at a time, you will feel a sense of accomplishment and a lot less stress. When looking at your outstanding balances, pay attention to how much interest you are paying monthly. If you are paying a lot in interest charges, consider looking for lower-interest options and consolidate all of your outstanding debts. Psychologically, it feels better to make one payment rather than many.

As a regular practice, balance your books on a monthly basis. Once you have a clear handle on what is available to save or spend, you can make choices from a position of strength. If you are not able to afford the things that you want in your life at this moment, keeping a clear vision of what it is that you want is the best incentive and easiest way to help you work towards achieving it.

Always feel gratitude for what you do have. Showing appreciation is an act of love and comes from your heart. It shouts to the universe that you want more of the same and it really does work to make you feel positive about what you have achieved as a result of your efforts. As described earlier, it is a good thing to do at the end of each day.

Set short-term, medium-term and long-term financial goals

When you have a PMA, you know what you want and focus your energy to achieve it. By looking at what you want this week, next month, in six months' time or in five years' time, you can develop a strategy to get there. If you look at your current thinking about your personal wealth, are you working towards something or just going through the motions because you have to survive? A PMA is looking beyond survival towards future pleasures.

Short-term financial goals

To help you set financial goals to serve your short-term needs, answer the following questions:

- Are you happy and comfortable where you are living?
- Is your job bringing in enough income to satisfy you?
- Do you have enough money to eat well?
- Do you have enough money to participate in leisure activities such as movies, theatre, holidays?
- Do you have enough money for the occasional treat?
- Is there anything you desire that would improve your current circumstances such as a computer or home renovation?
- How much more money do you want on a monthly basis to cover your immediate and short-term desires?

If you want better things for the present moment, work on the areas that may be easiest to achieve first, so number them accordingly. For each area, write down all the things you could do to solve the problem. Don't judge the answers or limit yourself – let your creative side take over. List-making should satisfy the logical thinkers, but don't be too logical. Don't rule out any possibilities because you don't think they are good enough, just write down what pops into your head. After you have written down your list, order the solutions by the easiest to implement first. Try them until you find one that works to solve the problem.

You might also want to consider the following options:

- Sell anything you don't want or need.
- Look at cutting back in some areas in order to use your money for things that bring you a bit of pleasure.
- Your home is probably your most valuable asset. If you want to improve it to make sure your investment doesn't devalue, it may be worthwhile talking to your lending institution.
- If you feel that you are undervalued at work, ask for a pay raise, or ask if there are other jobs available that pay more. If you don't ask, you will never know where you stand.

Once all your basic needs are met and you are able to feel relaxed with spending money and have fun in a responsible manner, you can begin to move towards more medium- and long-term goals like buying a bigger house or a new car or being able to start a family with security.

Medium-term financial goals

These are things that are not pressing, but you would like to have them some time in the next few years. It's great to plan ahead and work towards goals, but with every life experience you have, you are able to change the goal posts. Be sure not to get so rigid in your medium- to long-term plans that you forget to have fun along the way, or allow yourself to choose something different.

I am of the firm belief, and I'm sure you will agree, that the best way to make money is by doing something you really enjoy doing. Combining work and pleasure is the ultimate goal and, in my view, the key to wealth. When you are really passionate about something you do, you don't mind working at it. It is a labour of love and your enthusiasm and dedication will always be rewarded.

It's understandable that at some point in your life you may have to take any job that is available to meet your short-term needs. The beauty of planning for the future is that you can imagine what you would really like to do. The people that have the most earned wealth are often entrepreneurs, people who have ideas and put them into practice. Never be afraid to think big.

To set your medium-term goals, answer the following questions in as much detail as you can.

- Is there anything you would rather be doing to earn a living?
- Have you ever thought of setting up your own business?
- Would you rather be living in a different neighbourhood or a larger home?
- What things would you like to be able to do more of?
- What things would make your life more pleasurable?

Use the answers to these questions to begin thinking about how much money it would take to put them in practice. The more time you spend thinking and researching the possibilities, the more ideas you will get to help you achieve them.

Long-term financial goals

These generally relate to how you envision living your life after the age of retirement and can be a cause of worry the older you get. Good planning at an early age for the long-term future can help you to better enjoy all the stages of your life. Every little bit you put away early on earns interest and makes your money work for you. The ultimate goal is to reward yourself for all of your efforts with a life of comfort and pleasure. Thinking about the things that you would like to do, even if you are young, such as moving to a warmer climate, or travelling around the world, can keep you stimulated while you work towards achievement.

To attain long-term financial goals, answer the following questions.

- At what age would you like to retire?
- Where would you like to live?
- What activities would you like to pursue?
- What savings or investments have you made towards this end?
- How much wealth do you need to attract into your life to lead the life you want?

Your answers to these questions are the carrots at the end of the stick and the more you dream about them, want to achieve them and, most importantly, believe you can achieve them, the more likely you will be to find yourself getting there before you know it! There is no better time than today to start thinking about and planning what you want tomorrow.

Let's focus on happiness

I think that heading sums up how to develop a PMA about happiness in three words – FOCUS ON HAPPINESS. You don't have to have wealth, or even health, to find something that can make you feel happy in the moment. Long-term happiness is just practised moments of happiness – that easy. If you look for happiness, you can find signs of it everywhere, even by looking out a window. All it takes for you to find happiness is to find the little things, and they can be really small things, that bring you pleasure. Once you can bring yourself to a happy state of mind at any time, it will be easier to solve any problem or attain any goal. It also helps you to feel better on the physical level and with practice, will help you attract health and wealth into your life.

Everyone's definition of happiness will be different. My ideal of happiness is sitting on the beach in the Caribbean with the sun shining down and the crystal blue water beckoning me in for a swim. If you were afraid of water, this would be an absolute nightmare for you. The point is – no one can tell you how to be happy, or even what should make you happy, because you already know the feeling of happiness and what it takes to get you there. To attract happiness into your life, you have to be a happy bunny yourself.

The biggest hang-ups to happiness are:

- You think you don't deserve happiness.
- You dwell on things that don't make you feel good.
- You look at the worst in most situations.
- You take decisions that don't feel right.

You deserve happiness

At the end of the first chapter, you made a list of all the things you were proud of as a foundation on which to build your self-confidence. You know you are a good person with many wonderful traits and characteristics that make you the individual that you are. You have succeeded at many things and are loved by many people and these are just a few of the reasons that you deserve happiness. I know that when you think about it, you can list many, many more reasons for how you are a kind and loving person who deserves all the happiness in the world. When you are reliant on other people's approval to feel good about yourself, you are always wondering whether you are good enough. However, whenever you give anything you do your energy, attention and enthusiasm, you can't help but be the best you can be, so the worry is unnecessary and sets you back. By keeping your eye on the things you do well and giving them more and more of your attention you will find, almost immediately, that your feeling of self-worth grows on a daily basis.

To further develop your feelings of worthiness, try these simple exercises each night for a few weeks and see how much better they make you feel. It only takes a matter of minutes to make you feel good.

- As you prepare for bedtime, take a few minutes to look in the mirror and see all of your positive features. Look for ways to accentuate them in your choice of clothing, make-up or personal mannerisms.
- At the end of the day, write down all the things you accomplished. They don't have to be monumental; just every little thing you achieved in the day.

- Think about the acts of kindness you performed today.
- Think about the loving words you spoke today.

Find thoughts that make you feel good

We all have a bit of down time when things get on top of us. How long you choose to dwell on these feelings is always in your control. The more you dwell on them, the worse you will feel, so the simplest way to get out of a funk is to do something immediately that is good for you, and helps to lift your spirits. You have had so many happy moments in your life that you have lots of experience in knowing what works for you. For me, it's a scoop of my favourite ice cream or listening to music I can sing to – even though I have the worst voice in the world. Who cares – it's a great way to dispel bad feelings and raise your energy at the same time.

- Look at something beautiful. Beauty is always in the eye of the beholder, so find something close to hand that you believe to be beautiful. Whenever you look at beauty, either in nature, objects or people, it shows your capacity to love. This immediately opens up your heart and allows loving energy inside.
- Assemble an emergency feel-good collection that can immediately boost your spirits. Pick out some favourite music, funny movies, your favourite food or beverage, scents that uplift you, or activities you can do at a moment's notice that make you feel good. As soon as an unhappy thought enters your mind, choose to ignore it and do something constructive.
- Call upon an uplifting friend to help cheer you up. That is what friends are for!

Always look on the bright side of life

I know many people who go into each situation always look-ing at the worst things about it, and I always have such a difficult time understanding why. It guarantees you will feel bad, and 9 times out of 10, you live through a negative experience without any justifiable cause. Take, for example, the experience of going into a town to get something that you need. Your past experience might have indicated that you had a difficult time parking on some or even many occasions. In reality, today you may or may not have difficulty finding a space. If you worry about finding a space from the moment you know you have to go into town, how much time are you spending getting anxious and feeling bad? Worse still, the anticipation of a negative experience might prevent you from going into town at all. Why let your negative expectations limit your happiness and enjoyment? Wouldn't it feel better to be optimistic and think you have as good a chance as anyone else to get a parking space, and keep your eyes open for the possibilities? Looking on the negative side doesn't allow you to see all of the potential in a situation. Ever!

If you have a PMA, you always look at the best in people, places and things, and when you do that, you will find the best there is to find. It doesn't mean that every experience is going to be the best experience you ever had, but it does mean you will gain the maximum advantage from the situation.

See how you feel when you do this exercise. For each item, make a list of at least 10 positive things, and 10 more if you can.

- You
- Your partner (if you don't have one, think about 10 positive things that you would like to have in a partner)

- Your family
- Your home
- Your job
- Your friends
- Your community
- Your life

Doesn't it *feel* better to have positive thoughts and look at all the wonderful things that these situations add to your life?

I would like to share with you an exercise that I use daily, and often use it as an example when I am speaking to large groups of people. This is something that I learned from a dear friend in the States and I have used it successfully for many years. It may sound silly and you may be sceptical, but you won't know whether it works unless you try it! It emphasizes how expectations and faith can get you what you want!

This is a story about the parking angel; a very good friend of mine! Like the example we talked about earlier, negative expectations don't feel good and don't get you what you want most of the time, but expecting the best to happen feels good and helps you to further your desires.

Most of you, at some time, have a difficult time finding a parking space, especially if you are going into a busy city centre. Next time you are about to set out for your journey, when you get into your car, rather than getting stressed in advance, say this out loud:

'Parking angel, may I please have a parking space near . . . (be as specific as you can about where it is you would like to park). I would really appreciate anything you can do to help me and I thank you for anything you may be able to do.'

Set off on your way and see what happens. You will find that, in most cases (I usually find about 7 out of 10 times), there will be a space where you want it, even on the busiest day of the year. Remember to always say thank you, whether it works or not, for the efforts made on your behalf. The more it works, the more you will come to expect that it will always work and you increase your chances of success and feel good in the process.

Go with your gut instinct

Your instincts, or intuitive side, comprise your inner-self, the part of you that is deep down inside and knows what you really, really want and like based on the collective experiences you have had. Your instincts may reveal themselves as feelings or emotions, dreams or visions, or even something inexplicable. Sometimes you just know things. When you follow your instincts, you are using your PMA to trust that *you* know what is best to further your desires. If something feels good, go for it! If it doesn't feel right for any reason, no matter what other people may say, by trusting what you feel, you will always make the choice that is right for you at the time. The more you trust your instincts, the more you will be able to come to rely on them.

To see how your instincts help to guide you, answer the following questions:

● List any experiences where your instincts told you one thing, but you did something else. How did things turn out?

- When have you followed your instincts and it turned out well?
- What do your instincts tell you to do to achieve happiness?
- According to your instincts, what is the next move forward in your life?
- What have your instincts told you about the people you have met?
- What have your instincts told you about your health?
- Have you ever won anything based on a gut instinct?

Look at your answers and see how your instincts have guided you in past decisions. Look at how your instincts tell you to be happy and follow your own best advice.

Hang around with happy people

In every situation, always look at the happiest people to spend your time with. Happy people have discovered how to enjoy life to the fullest, and you can benefit by going along for the ride! They know how to find the best in all situations and you can learn, through their experiences, a far happier outlook on life. Who do you know in your personal and professional life that is happy most of the time? Next time you think about whom to spend your time with, draw upon the happy people in your life.

I have used all of the following techniques to help people successfully find joy and happiness in more areas of their lives. Before starting any of these techniques, find the most comfortable spot available to sit and relax and always begin by quieting your mind by concentrating on your breathing, remembering to keep your shoulders relaxed. Take a deep breath in to the count of five, and out slowly to the count of five. Repeat this 3 to 5 times until you begin to feel relaxed. Not everyone will have the same experience with visualizations, but it doesn't matter at all. Some of you may be able to see it clearly in your mind's eye. Others may not be so visual and may see it through a mist or fog, or others may not be able to see it all, but may feel the experience in other ways. It only takes a few minutes to begin to feel better.

This is great for pain relief or for a quick pick-me-up when you are feeling out of sorts.

The perfect getaway

I want you to think about the one spot in the world, wherever that may be, that you are always at your happiest. Try to get as detailed as you can, thinking about the journey it may take to get there, what the temperature may be like, or the activities going on around you. Think about all the things you love to do in your favourite place and of the happy times you have spent there. As you begin to relax, you feel an overwhelming sense of lightness and joy at being in such a lovely place. You can stay in this place as long as you like, and know that this is a place you can go to anytime you want to feel better. When you are ready to leave, slowly bring your awareness to your physical body. Shake your feet out a few times and begin to wriggle your toes. As you begin to open your eyes, remember what it feels like to be happy and know that you are a happy, fun-loving person who would like to have more of the same.

This one is great for overcoming negative feelings about your physical body. You can also send this loving energy to someone else, by thinking of him or her, rather than you receiving the energy.

Love your body

How you begin this exercise will depend upon how you feel when you do it. If you are lacking in energy, start from your feet up. If you have nervous energy or find it difficult to relax, start from your head down. If you have any particular part of your body that you don't like or that doesn't feel good in the moment, spend extra time in that area.

Imagine the most beautiful shade of green that you can think of and focus on this lovely colour that symbolizes love and growth. Think of all the beautiful shades of green that you see in nature, and that in order for things to grow they need love and attention. Begin either at your feet or at your head, and imagine a ball of beautiful green light is entering your body. As it reaches each part of your body, you are able to feel the warmth of the love that this energy brings. Stay on each part for about 30 seconds, or until it feels right to move on. Spend several minutes in any area that needs special attention. As the energy begins to travel towards your heart, you are able to feel an enormous flow of love into your heart. It may even bring tears of joy to your eyes as your remember all the love that you have in your life. When you complete sending this loving energy throughout your body, know that you are a wonderful person on the inside and that whenever you let the love shine through, you are the most beautiful person on the earth. When you feel that you are ready, slowly start to shake out your hands and wriggle your toes. Slowly open your eyes and keep in the spirit of love.

Attracting wealth

Imagine that you have just received a phone call telling you that you have won a sum of money large enough that you can put into place your greatest desire. Think about how excited you feel knowing that your dreams can now become a reality. Think about the first things you would do after getting the news. Imagine all the steps you would take to implement your desire. If it is having a bigger house, imagine in great detail the neighbourhood, the amount of rooms and layout. If it is having a new, big plasma television, see yourself watching it and enjoying the experience of having what you want. Whatever financial desires that money can buy, see yourself as having and enjoying the experience in as great a detail as possible. When you feel comfortable in the experience, slowly bring your awareness back to your physical body and wriggle your toes and fingers. Slowly open your eyes and remember how good it felt to have all that you want. Ask the universe for the abundance you desire and have faith that you will be guided in ways to find what you desire.

5.

Building on Your Success

Success is *any* movement in a positive direction. It doesn't matter how small a step it may be towards the big picture, as each step forward that you take makes you a stronger and happier person. What your definition of success is will vary from everyone else's so other people's success isn't a standard to judge by. It can help you to determine some of the things that you may want in life and, for that reason, it is good to look at successful people. However, if you judge your own success by other people's standards, you won't be true to yourself. This is especially the case in your relationship with your parents if your ideals differ from theirs. Although they may have the most wonderful of intentions in wanting the best for you, at some point, based on your own experiences, you determine what your own definition of success will be. The bottom line is, you make your own success by sticking to the things you know you want, and always wanting more. There is never a time to rest on your successes, as the moment you do so, you stop summoning the desire to accomplish anything new. Even in retirement, when you may want to give up some of the areas that you have previously achieved in, by desiring success in everything you do, it will be a far easier and more enjoyable experience.

You build on your success by looking at the small achievements, and knowing that if you continue doing the same thing, you will reach your ultimate goal. A good example is looking at how to build on your success with any weight-loss programme. You know your current weight and you have an idea where you want to end up and, depending upon how far away the difference between the two may be, there can be a big difference in how long it takes to get there. If you look at the big picture, of perhaps wanting to reduce your clothing by a few sizes, it can seem overwhelming and the slow progress that you may make in the beginning could dishearten you. But if you look at the progression of the weight loss, like a zipper being easier to close, this small step can feel like a giant leap forward and spur you on to achieve your ideal body weight. Recognizing small achievements feels great and provides an incentive to keep going. Once you see a successful result, sticking with the programme will continue to work for you.

We all like to be rewarded for doing something successfully because it allows us to feel appreciation: an enormously positive, loving feeling in your heart. When you feel appreciated, it helps you to know on a deeper level that your efforts are worthwhile and that you are on the right path to get your desired results. We often seek appreciation or rewards from those we look up to – perhaps partners, parents or our superiors at work – and can be let down if our efforts go unnoticed. However, it is far more important for you to feel good about your own accomplishments than to rely on others, because the control is back in your hands. You have the ability to acknowledge every small success on a personal level and the most important thing for you to remember is that if you did it once, you can do it again. Successes stay with you forever. Once you are proud of yourself, you will exhibit such great confidence that you will take on the next challenge.

There are many ways to reward yourself. The easiest way to get excited about an achievement is to tell someone else about it – not necessarily to get positive feedback, but to shout to the world that you can do what you set your mind to do. Think about the joy of telling your parents about good grades in a school report. You felt great that you did it, but you also wanted your family and friends to know because you were proud of your efforts. As I sit here writing this book, and every other book I write, I set a daily target of how many words I want to write. With the wonders of technology, I am able to tell how many words I have written in less than a second, and this always spurs me on. I often send emails to my husband with word-count updates, to show him how well I am doing. The more I write, the more I want to write and when I am on a roll, I can triple my daily goal, just by acknowledging my success in the minute. The next time you do something you are proud of, think about sharing it with a friend.

Writing things down is the best way to keep track of pretty much anything in your life. When you see something written down, it is much easier to remember it.

Keeping a diary of the small successes you have on a daily basis is another way of helping to build your self-esteem and give you a sense of accomplishment at the end of the day. It also makes for very good reading when you are having a down time and wonder about where you are going. Looking back on all the things you have done well can help to motivate and inspire you to get back on track. The more detail you write about how you achieved the success, the more useful the diary will be to remind you of the steps you took to get there. It also serves as a way of quickly being able to update your CV.

Another way to reward yourself is to give yourself a treat – something special that you may not do often enough. During the course of the day, when you have successfully accomplished a task you set out to do, give yourself a pat on the back. Go out for a coffee or plan to meet a friend in the evening. When you have accomplished something around the house, relax and put your feet up or have a hot soak in the tub. Learning to associate enjoyable things with accomplishing your goals makes working on them more of a pleasure. Think of the benefits of planning a holiday in the future. Not only do you experience the excitement long before you get there, but the thought of the reward makes you work harder to achieve you goal. It also can make the time go by more quickly and enjoyably in the process.

In other words, the more excited you get about achieving even a very small step in the right direction, the more you realize that you like that feeling and want more of the same. Success breeds confidence which breeds success – a positive on-going cycle if you take the time to clock each success and make the most of them.

Behind every successful person, there are many helpers along the way

Whereas appreciating your own success is really important in helping to build on your self-esteem, acknowledging that behind your success are the people that encourage, support or teach you things, is a way of always having continuing support from them. Thanking every single member of the team, down to those people that made your life bearable in the process of achieving your success, will make them feel important and more willing to help out and try their all in the future. Unless you are able to say thank you, it is unlikely that you will receive many thanks in return.

I can tell you that, as a teacher, there is nothing in the world more gratifying than a letter of thanks from a student. I feel such an enormous sense of almost motherly pride in seeing someone learn something new and advance on their personal path, as well as my own sense of achievement for having taught them well. I always write back and let them know how much their appreciation was appreciated to continue the cycle of feeling good. Giving thanks is the surest way of continued success. You know the old saying – what goes around, comes around – well, in the case of gratitude I certainly believe it is true.

It is not just those directly involved in your success who require appreciation. Sometimes, in order to be successful, you have to rely on others to pick up the slack, as can often be the case if you have a high-pressure job. It may mean that you have to work long hours, maybe even on weekends, and that cuts into your personal time, often leaving those closest to you to shoulder additional responsibilities. This is most often the case with your family, where partners or children may suffer by not seeing you as much or not having you around to shoulder some of the responsibilities at home. By actively letting them know how much their support means to you, it can make them feel more special in helping to contribute to the overall family goals.

- When was the last time you thanked:
    Someone who works for or with you?
    Someone you work for?
    A loved one?
    A stranger – for example a shop assistant?
- Do you always thank people when they are considerate?

Learn from your success

In order for you to have achieved your desired goal, you had to take action to get there. Whether it was as simple as getting the groceries when you needed them, or finishing up a complicated project, you knew what you wanted, committed your time and energy and had the motivation to achieve it. In the process you found an efficient system of working to your highest advantage. It could be by getting up earlier and fitting in something before you go off to work, or finding that you think best after a good meal, but to have achieved your success you had to have the right set of ingredients that worked for you.

In order to make it easier to duplicate your successes in the future more easily, it is good to understand your preferences to see how to build a model of success for all areas of your life. By incorporating your preferences into all you undertake, you start out with a game plan for how best to succeed.

Answer these questions to understand more about your general tendencies:

- Are you a morning or night person?
- What time of the day are you most alert?
- Do you like to do things alone or when people are around?
- Do you like to work in silence or have noise around you?
- Do you like to do things at the same time each day?
- Do you make lists?
- What motivates you?

Look at your successful work habits:

- Do you understand things better with words or pictures?
- Are you better doing research and writing or presenting ideas?
- Are you better at the big picture or in the details?

- Are you better with one big project, or lots of little ones?
- Are you better leading or following?
- Do you work better under pressure or with long lead times?
- Are you more logical or creative?
- Do you work better from the office or from your home?
- Are you better working for yourself or for others?

Look at your successful personal relationships:

- Do you like people who:
  Work in the same profession or do something different?
  Share or have different interests?
  Like to be active or homebodies?
  Are older, younger, or the same age?
- Do you prefer to look after people, or be looked after?

What's next?

The best time to begin a new challenge is with a success under your belt. Starting from a position of great confidence serves you well and provides the impetus for you to have more of the feelings and benefits of being successful.

By looking ahead to the next challenge, you look to rise to the next level of your personal development. To achieve this, you may have to take on additional responsibilities or seek further education, and in the desire to have greater success, you will be motivated to do what it takes.

Some people use their success to further themselves on the same path. If you are a great teacher, you may desire to be a head teacher or, if you are a sales assistant, you may want to be retail manager. There are many advances that are within reach in your own profession that can provide the stimulus to keep you interested and excited. Letting those in a more superior position know that you are keen to advance will help you to find out what you need to achieve to get there. Looking for ways to expand your interest and knowledge about your key area will help to keep your ideas flowing and will help you to generate new ideas, which in turn makes you more valuable at what you do. If you enjoy the security of knowing what is expected of you and, most importantly, really enjoy your chosen path, this is the best way forward for you.

You may also want to think about:

- Does your company offer any suitable personal development programmes?
- Is there another company in your field of experience that you would rather work for?
- Are there other geographic locations that you would like to work in?
- Are you marketable enough to go out on your own?

From a broader perspective, success at one thing gives you the confidence to explore new areas where you can exploit your many other talents. You are a multi-talented individual who has natural and developed abilities. Because you have always been successful at one thing, doesn't mean that you are stuck doing the same thing for the rest of your life. When you have discovered that success is a state of mind – meaning *whatever* you really focus your energy and attention on, you have an inner knowing that even if you haven't done it before you will succeed – over the course of your lifetime you can be successful at many different things. Once you reach that realization, and I truly hope that time is now, you will never again be fearful of trying anything you want to do. I can think of at least ten different types of jobs I have done that are mostly unrelated, although in some cases, one has led to another in the same field. Some were through advancement, and others were through pursuing a job that sounded interesting, even though I had never tried it before. When you have success in one area, it is easy to persuade anyone that you have the ability to see things through, which generally leads to success on any employer's bottom line. The more you are able to talk about your success and your other abilities with confidence, which should be easy based on your success so far, the more convincing you will be that you are competent to do it.

Remember, if you're not in the game, you can't win!

- List all the skills that you are required to use on a daily basis.
- Think of all the ways you can utilize these skills to do something completely different.
- List all the other natural or learned abilities you have
- What professional courses have you taken?
- Do you put these skills into practice?
- Think of other areas where your skills can be utilized.
- Is there something you have always wanted to try your hand at?

Success in one part of your life can help you in another

With all the work you have done on developing a positive mental attitude, transferring the success from one area of your life to another makes perfect sense. Because success feels good and puts you in a positive frame of mind, you are more likely to have a positive frame of mind in other things you do. For example, if you have a really happy personal life, when you get up in the morning, on most occasions, you are in a happy and confident mood, knowing that your personal life is in good order. You are more likely to be able to concentrate on your job as there are fewer worrying thoughts occupying your mind. You can also look at the case of the weight-loss programme – if you are able to successfully achieve your goals by losing weight, and as a result feel more confident and attractive, the success generated in this area of your life will have positive influences in both your social and professional life.

I often hear people say, 'If only I had this . . . I could do that . . .' referring to whatever is getting in the way of a particular goal or objective. Other common excuses are: 'If I had his money, I could do . . .' or, 'If only I was prettier, I could do . . .', 'Because I don't have a degree, I can't achieve . . .' and so the list continues. Therefore, striving to achieve the first step in order to have the overall success you desire is a good thing.

To find out where to get the ball of success rolling, look at the areas of your life that you feel need to be sorted before you are able to achieve your overall goals. Number them in order of importance, with 1 being the most important.

- Physical fitness
- Appearance

- Intelligence
- Money
- Love life
- Children/family
- Home
- Other

Start with the one thing that you believe is preventing you from achieving overall success in your life. Write down 10 ways that it would be possible to overcome it. Don't judge your answers on how realistic you think they may be; look at all the possibilities, whether you think they are good or bad. When you have written down 10, try to think of 10 more. When you have written down all of the ways that you can think of that would be possible to achieve that goal, number your answers, beginning with the easiest and best method to try first.

Let's look at 20 ways to be more successful in attracting a loving relationship into your life:

- Pursue interests that you would like to attract in a partner, such as dancing, fitness, or speaking a foreign language.
- Socialize more.
- Ask friends if they can fix you up.
- Travel on your own.
- Get fit.
- Have a make-over.
- Be less rigid in your ideals – open up to possibilities.
- Learn to flirt.
- Tell someone you are interested in that you like them.
- Think about the characteristics you want in a lover/ partner.

- Feel deserving of love.
- List your loving qualities and practise them.
- Be on the lookout for someone you feel attracted to.
- Try new things, such as going a different way to work, and eating in different places.
- Seek companionship first and see what happens.
- Plan a party and ask guests to bring someone new.
- Place a personal ad in a paper you read regularly.
- Try speed-dating with the intention of having a laugh.
- Be aware of your body language – are you approachable?
- Dress for success.

You can try out one item on your list each day, or try them in any combination. However you do it, it gets you taking positive action to help you with a goal that makes a big difference in your life. Hopefully, you have at least 20 ways to get going and take the first step. Nothing ventured – nothing gained.

Turn success into cash

I have a very entrepreneurial spirit and have always found ways to turn some of my talents into cash. To help put myself through university back in the early 70s, I used to embroider jeans with elaborate scenes in my spare time. I started a cottage industry of hand-knitters to produce a line of jumpers that I designed and sold throughout the States. I have made jewellery for over 30 years and teach and practise Reiki as a source of income. I also founded a chain of retail stores based in the UK that specialized in products to help you store and organize your material possessions, as a result of not being able to find this service in the UK when I first moved here. Turning your successful skills, passions and talents into a source of revenue is much easier than you think.

Over the years that I have lived in England, I have met and employed many people who have started a business based on something they love. I have a lovely dog-walker who, in his native Brazil, cared for some of the many homeless dogs that wander the streets. I have used amazing seamstresses who have turned their skills to generate cash from home while they are looking after their family. I have had gorgeous food prepared by enterprising young chefs starting out on their own and have so many friends who make their living through art, music, floristry, gardening and complementary therapies that I know that if you really want to make a success of turning your talents to profits, you really can!

Starting a small business on your own doesn't usually take too much capital, and if you are not ready to give up the day job, you can always do it in conjunction with another job as a way to earn extra cash. In this technological age, it is easier than ever to market your services with little effort through using home computers to generate brochures or marketing materials or using the Internet as a way to drum up some business. It is also a great way to test market potential to see if there is enough interest to do it full time.

As with anything, the more time you spend thinking about something, or researching its potential, the more excited you will get, so although you may have an initial fear of stepping out on your own, the exhilaration of doing something daring that you know you want to do is worth every moment of the doubts you may have initially. You feel most alive when you are doing something that you really love and enjoy, so as long as you do the initial planning, you will have the confidence to give it a go. The most important part of being a successful businessperson is having the ability to market and shout loudly about your skills.

Many people write to me as a result of watching *The Life Laundry* who are organized and able to help people sort things out. I always try to be a mentor and suggest ways they can put their skills to good use as a means of income and I am pleased to say that I hear about many of their successes. These are some of the key factors you can consider and implement to help you on your way.

- Do you need to purchase equipment to start up? If so, get details on costs. Look at ways of financing the purchase, if required.
- Do you need any licences or insurance?
- Is there anyone you would like to go into business with?
- Are there many people who do what you do in your area?
- How much do they charge for their services?
- How do your skills differ from those of others?
- In general, whom do you think needs your services?
- Do you know anyone that needs your services?
- What are the best ways to reach them?
- How much income would you desire to make it a worthwhile effort?
- Do you think it has potential to expand?
- How would you expand it in the future?
- Are there any trade associations that can help you market your services?
- Are there any local/national grants or support to help?

- Is there anyone you can ask for advice or financial help if you need it?
- Do you have a good relationship with your bank?

Here are some great ways to market local businesses.

- Local newspapers always love to report on new things going on. All it takes is writing a press release announcing your services or calling and asking for a chat with the features editor of your local paper.
- Demonstrate your skills. Participate in relevant local activities, even if it means doing it for free. The more you get used to presenting things to larger groups, the more likely you are to find interested participants.
- Look at your uniqueness and see if there are any national publications that may have an interest in what you do. Go to the newsstand and browse through the numerous special interest publications and see where you fit in.
- Local radio reaches lots of people in a concentrated geographic area so try to exploit your skills through a local station. Can you be a local expert on a topic of interest?
- Are there any local companies that would recommend your services?
- Put interesting brochures out at local grocery stores, hair salons or restaurants if allowed.
- Get recommendations from past clients and ask if they would be willing to speak to other people about their experience if required.
- Take out advertisements in relevant publications.
- Link with relevant websites.
- Print business cards and always keep them to hand.

Start small and get success under your belt, but never, ever be afraid to think big. Just because you don't have it now, doesn't mean that you are never going to get it. Think as big as you want and see it happening. If you dedicate yourself to spending the time it may take to get the venture off the ground – and it could be some time – and still continue to love and enjoy it, it will be a guaranteed success.

Big picture considerations:

- Total resources needed
- Does it require borrowing or bringing in investors?
- Can you keep control of the venture?
- Can you manage the leap from small to medium or even larger?
- Will it require even more work?
- At what point does it stop being fun?
- If you can do it once, you can do it again.

Can you ever have too much success?

This is an interesting question, and in some cases the answer can be yes. If you are very successful, perhaps a leader in your field, and have been successful for a long time, the outside world may have expectations for you to further succeed. This can be true of your employer, your family, the press and, most importantly, yourself. Perhaps you can relate this to your childhood when your parents or teachers wanted you to do better than you already had – even if you were at the top of the form. Because you did well, they wanted to see if you could do better still to reach your maximum potential. The intentions are sincere, but sometimes it can make you feel pressurized to not disappoint those around you.

The benefits of your success may be an improved lifestyle for you or your family, so the financial rewards of your success put pressure on you to drive forward. As you always have to put in the time in order to be successful, it often means that you and your family have made sacrifices to achieve the level of comfort your success has made possible. Out of a sense of obligation to look after your family in a manner to which they are accustomed, you continue to work and sacrifice things you would rather have to maintain the lifestyle.

Those that are successful on a national or international level suffer the loss of their privacy as a result. They live their lives through the lens of a camera and can become distrusting and reclusive as a result. Everyone is fascinated by the ability of an individual to rise to great heights and wants to know how they got there, what they do to stay there, or what are their future plans. The pressure to be perfect must be enormous, and only the strong-hearted are impervious to these negative effects of too much success. When you are held in high esteem, it is easy to feel that there is a long way to fall if you don't continue to prove yourself.

As a result of your success you will probably have some critics who do not value your contribution as much as others. Criticism is good and valid and it allows you to grow at whatever you do, providing you accept it for what it is: the opinion of a person you either respect or don't. If you respect the person's opinion, you need to heed the advice given and take on board any changes to improve on your successful endeavours. If the criticism is given with other motives in mind, let it go, as focusing on it is surely a way to make you lose time or even confidence in your ability to continue to perform well.

If you put yourself under too much pressure, your body may tell you it is time to relax. The stress on your body can manifest in tense muscles, elevated blood pressure or more serious heart dis-ease. The need to succeed can also take its toll on your mental abilities to think, concentrate and produce. Without allowing your mind and physical body the ability to recharge and relax, your success in some or many areas of your life are unlikely to continue. Unless you are unable to experience new things and broaden your perspective by taking time off, it will be very difficult to come up with new and stimulating ideas. Those who continually succeed stay ahead of the game by refreshing, experiencing and imagining new things all the time.

When success gets on top of you, it's time to gain some perspective. Think about the crock of gold at the end of the rainbow that you were trying to achieve.

- Has your success in one area placed other areas in your life out of balance?
- Have you got there yet?
- Is there something that you would still like to achieve in this area?
- Have the goal posts changed?
- What is the thing that you like most about your success?
- Are there other ways to get the same feeling?
- What's next?

Can you successfully manage a career and a family?

Anyone can 'manage' anything, so the answer is probably yes, you can successfully manage a career and family. Whether you enjoy doing it depends upon the reasons that you choose to do both. If it is because both things hold great importance to you in your life, as you want to do them for personal satisfaction, I believe you can create an ideal work situation that enables you to advance your career and dedicate time to your family and household. If you do it out of financial necessity, as many must do, there is a slight change in the motivation between wanting to do something and having to do something. When you feel you have to do something, it indicates you would rather be doing something else, in which case there is often a bit of resentment involved in having to do it, making it difficult to focus on either the job or the family. In either case, organization is the key to being able to do both more successfully.

The 'art' of managing is the ability to oversee many things at one time, without letting them clutter your mind and cause confusion. To effectively delegate tasks and responsibilities to others, you must be able to clearly communicate what needs to be done. If you put in a bit of time at the outset in planning the jobs that need to be shared, then once you pass on the responsibilities your mind will be clear to focus on your share of the tasks. Writing things down is a good way to make sure everyone has something to work towards.

Getting the whole family, even young children, to participate in maintaining household routines will teach everyone the value of teamwork in achieving a common goal.

Make a note of who will be responsible for the following:

- Cooking
- Shopping
- Laundry
- Cleaning the bathroom
- Cleaning the lounge
- Cleaning the kitchen

- Putting the rubbish out
- Changing the linen
- Vacuuming
- Paying the bills
- Looking after pets, if applicable

To get into a routine, the easiest way to go about it is to schedule everything at the same time, daily or weekly, depending upon the task. Drawing a chart of all the activities, according to everyone's schedule, will help to get the basics done so that you can all enjoy quality relaxation time together at the end of the day.

If you have young children, coordinating day care and school runs if you are working full time will probably require additional help. The more organized you are at planning a weekly schedule of who needs to be where and when, the fewer interruptions you will have during your working day.

- Assign an area of your home for all paperwork relating to schedules and activities and make sure everyone uses it on a daily basis.
- Make a weekly schedule of activities and put it in a place that is easily accessible. A chalkboard is easy to maintain, or paint a wall with chalkboard paint to make it fun.
- Look at ways of sharing help. Friends with children of a similar age can pool resources to cut down on expenses.
- Explore flexible working hours, like starting later in the morning to get kids off to school. If possible, look at ways your partner may be able to start earlier and leave earlier in order to have more time with your children.

If you would rather be home with your kids, but need the income, it is a good time to spread your wings and look at ways of generating income while still being at home during the key hours of the day when your children are around. All it takes is a bit of creative problem-solving to find a solution that can work for you. Looking at solutions always feels better than staying stuck doing something you don't want to be doing.

- How much income do you want to generate?
- How much income do you currently generate?
- How many hours do you work?
- Can you work evenings or weekends?
- Can you work longer hours on fewer days?
- If applicable, can you do your current work from home?
- What skills do you have that can turn your success into cash?

Success *can* go to your head

When success goes to your head, it often bypasses your heart, and it is easy to forget your humanity. The constant drive for success is a very self-focused desire that can leave many people behind in its wake. It can also represent a need to continually prove to yourself and the world that you are good enough.

When you live in your head, you are often unaware of the things that go on around you. You may have lots of nervous energy and find it difficult to relax as you are always thinking about the next challenge. When you achieve the balance of living in your heart and taking actions as a result of how you feel, you remain more centred in your approach. Success is about having it all – wealth, health and happiness.

When you think back to all the things that you wanted as a result of your success:

- Have you taken the time to enjoy them?
- Do you appreciate the people that stood by you?
- Do you feel satisfied with what you have achieved?
- Do you feel that you still have something to prove?
- Do you continue to see the same social group as you did before you had your success?
- What's the best thing about having your success?

6.
Speak Up

'Our opinions do not really blossom into fruition until
we have expressed them to someone else.'

Mark Twain

One of the biggest causes of mental clutter is having thoughts
and feelings that you are unable to express. Issues that you
have on your mind can consume your thoughts and prevent
you from fully experiencing what is happening in the moment.
Until you release those thoughts by communicating them,
they will go unresolved and continue to hold you back. Gaining the confidence to say what you feel will keep your mind
clear and focused to help you get what you want out of life.

The biggest factor in being unable to say what is on your
mind is the fear of rejection. You worry that what you have
to say is not worthy enough, or that your feelings will not be
reciprocated. It is a fear that we all face in some personal and
professional circumstances. This fear may be rooted in a past
experience when you were unable to clearly express your
point of view.

The biggest problem with fear is that each time you hold
back from doing something out of fear, the fear grows. By
learning to effectively communicate, you can begin to express
your opinions more confidently, starting with less emotional
topics, and once you see how easy it is and how good it feels
to release your thoughts, you will be able to face the more

emotional issues that you need to express. By speaking up, you will always know where you stand.

Many creatures in the animal kingdom use their ability to communicate to maintain their existence. Animals warn of danger, signal intention to mate, and indicate sources of food by signalling their knowledge or physical needs through sound. If you have domestic pets like dogs and cats, you understand what they want and like from their ability to express their preferences to you in their own language. From the moment you came into this world shouting to have your needs met, you exercised your natural ability to communicate your needs to those around you. As you were learning to speak, you probably pointed to things that you wanted and learned the words to enable you to get them when you wanted them. When you stop voicing your desires, there is no way to get them, other than waiting for the world to read your mind.

There are many non-verbal ways that we signal our feelings and preferences, but they are always subject to interpretation. You may yawn or look away from someone who is boring you, or tighten up the muscles in your face if you don't agree with what someone is saying, or even cry, out of frustration or sadness, but if the other person is unaware of how you are feeling, you will continue to be plagued by experiences you do not enjoy. It is often the fear of upsetting others or not fitting in with those around you that prevents you from speaking your mind.

The truth is, it is never what you say; it is all in how you say it. You can deliver the worst piece of news, and if it is from your heart, you will always find the words to express it in the best possible way.

It is sometimes difficult to overcome a cultural upbringing that teaches you not to speak until you are spoken to, or that it's better to be seen and not heard. These are probably phrases that you remember from your childhood when your parents also wanted you to learn the rules of listening and assimilating information before speaking too quickly. It is a way of learning to value other people's opinions in order to filter those opinions through the collection of your own experiences and judge whether you agree or disagree with them. This is the way that we all learn new ideas. Taken quite literally, however, you can believe that you are so insignificant that your opinion has no value. Without the birth of new ideas, the universe would never solve any of the problems of the world, and it all starts with the expression of personal thought. Although everything you say may not dramatically impact on the world, it surely will impact on how you feel in your own world.

Throughout this book, you can see how the life experiences of your parents and their parents before them have influenced your thoughts, beliefs, attitudes and habits, and in order to express your individuality as you were growing up, you had to voice your own opinions about many of the things you were taught. You spoke up about the food you wanted to eat, things you wanted to study, clothes you wanted to wear, people you wanted to date and activities you wanted to participate in, and this gave you confidence to act on your own inner feelings about what is best for you. It may not have made you the most popular member of the family, but you probably felt true to yourself.

If you found it difficult to go against the wishes of your parents then, you may have needed their approval, which is easy to get by thinking in the same way as them. Everyone likes validation that their own ideas are good and valuable, and when you agree with someone, it massages their ego. You may continue to quietly fit in because you continue to believe that the best way for continuing approval is to do as other people want and expect you to do. But it is my belief, based on all the cases that I have seen, that whenever you go against your own nature – what you truly believe and want deep down inside – you will always feel a sense of loss for what might have been.

Your voice represents your degree of confidence in what you have to offer. There may be many areas of your life where you are happy to share your thoughts with those around you; those are areas where you are sure of what you want or believe in and are most likely to find success. Any area of your life where your thoughts are manifested from words into action, will make you feel a sense of completion. This is a cycle of energy that continues to flow – new ideas are talked about, adapted on occasion through the input of others, then put into action, and the trough is emptied once again to receive the new ideas.

Cat got your tongue?

Look at the following areas of your life and see where you are really tongue-tied, either through confusion or fear of looking foolish or being rejected. Think about the one thing you want to express in each relevant area and write it down, directing your thoughts towards the person you want to address.

If you can approach each area from your personal vantage point of how the situation makes *you* feel, you will take responsibility for your feelings and seek clarification from the other party, which is far less threatening to them. When you blame others for your feelings, you relinquish your control and put others in the position of having to defend their actions, which is far more threatening to them and makes a favourable resolution less likely.

Situation	*Confusion*	*Fear*
Romantic relationships		
Work environment		
Children		
Extended family		
Household matters		
Health		
Money		

Once you are able to crystallize and verbalize your thoughts, it is far easier to deal with them. Getting them down on paper allows you the emotional release which enables you to look at them more realistically and take the next step, and let your voice be heard. Make sure that you stick to the one point you want to raise, and don't go back to old history, which confuses the issue and brings it back to an emotional level. Solve a problem one step at a time.

Here are some good communication practices.

- Set an agenda
- Stick to the point
- Never interrupt another person's thoughts
- Listen
- Think before you speak
- Take notes, if appropriate
- Ask the other person what they would do if they were you.

In this age of technology, we live in a world of instant communication, where we can contact people across the globe in just a few seconds. It is easier than ever to find the right way for you to put your inner thoughts out there and feel a sense of resolution in knowing where you stand. Look at the following ways to tackle each of the problem areas you listed above and choose the easiest and best method to address your concerns. The ultimate goal is to attain a resolution of the problem to enable you to feel better and move forward as a result of knowing where you stand.

Interactive – Quick response – Clearest outcome

Face-to-face

Although for many this might be the most difficult option, the most immediate way to get feedback and know where you stand is by having a one-to-one conversation. When you meet with someone face-to-face, you are able to best judge their response not only by what they say, but by looking into their eyes and seeing how they feel as well. You know what they say – the eyes are the windows to the soul. If practicable, it should always be the first choice to help you resolve things faster and more satisfactorily.

Try to plan ahead and, if possible, pick a time of the day that you feel at your best. If you are raring to go in the morning and like to get things off your chest at the start of the day, see if it is convenient for that person to see you at that time of the day. If you feel it is appropriate, let the person know what you want to discuss. In a business setting, read any papers that may be required and get them to the person in enough time for them to be able to prepare in advance of getting together. It is the best way of resolving things in one meeting.

Try to choose a location for the meeting that is most conducive for you to put across your thoughts. If you are intimidated by your boss's office and want to get something resolved, suggest meeting in your office or get together over a coffee. If you want to bring something up with a partner, find a space that you know both of you like and plan to chat there. The fewer the distractions, the better able you are to concentrate on what is being said, as well as what you want to say.

Take some time at the end of your face-to-face to sum up what has been said and resolved so there is no further confusion on the subject. If it requires further action, set a date for it to be started and clarify who needs to take the action to put the matter to rest. If appropriate, take notes and write them up for all involved.

Make sure to look and feel your best before any important meeting – business or personal. Get lots of sleep; eat right on the day and dress for a successful outcome.

Interactive – Quick-Medium response – Less certain outcome

Telephone

The telephone is a good option to transcend time and space, and it can also provide immediate feedback, although with less clarity than a face-to-face as you are not able to see people's reactions to what you are saying. It is not possible to judge whether you have the recipient's undivided attention as there are many distractions such as computers, paperwork or other people around that can also occupy their mind at the same time.

Speaking on the telephone de-personalizes the experience,

and for many, it can be easier than saying things face-to-face. The benefits of a telephone conversation are that you can easily write things down to help you better understand what the other person is saying and you have less worries about your physical appearance that may enable you better to focus on what you have to say. In that your voice is the integral way that you are able to transmit your feelings about the situation over the telephone, taking care to watch the tone of your voice in a telephone conversation is an important element. Remember, it is not necessarily what you say, but how you say it, that will leave the lasting impression. Try to maintain a conversational tone throughout your conversation and keep as much emotion out of your voice as you can.

If possible, the telephone is a better choice for resolving non-personal problems than for issues that have emotional consequences. It is a good choice to resolve business matters and for information gathering. If you want to resolve business matters, it is best to plan the call and, as with a face-to-face, send appropriate paperwork well in advance of the meeting. In the case of resolving issues such as technical support questions or billing matters, be sure to have all the relevant documentation to hand prior to making the call. Write down the time, date and person you spoke with in order to have a record of your discussion for further action needed. Be sure to sum up your understanding of the resolution of the issues at the end of your conversation to keep tabs on future action that may be needed to conclude the matter. Write a date in your notes when follow-up action needs to be taken.

The telephone is often a more spontaneous means of communicating and it is very easy to pick it up without thinking about the consequences of your actions. Although it is a fantastic way to keep in touch with those you care about or need to speak with, the immediacy and the degree of anonymity of the medium can cause you to speak before you think. Whenever you have the urge to purge, take a few minutes to gather your thoughts before you pick up the phone.

Non-interactive – Uncertain time frame – Unresolved outcome

Write a letter

With the advent of e-mail and text messaging, the art of letter writing is a skill that is lost to many. It is often easier to write in a new form of shorthand where it is speed rather than thought that drives the message. 'How R U?' or 'LOL' replace the more thoughtful versions, and although it is good fun to be able to communicate upbeat and happy, quick thoughts to friends or family, they should rarely be used to solve more complex issues.

Writing a letter to resolve a problem helps to release some of the emotion. It also serves to leave an historical document of your thoughts, feelings or experiences at a particular point in time. It is a thoughtful process where you can carefully phrase what you want to get across and fully express your side of the story. You can choose the manner in which it is accepted by how you choose to write it. A handwritten letter is always more personal and should always be used to express thoughts of a personal nature. You may choose to write your thoughts in a card that may be an eye-catching way to express what you are feeling. Business letters will attract more attention if they are typewritten. In all cases, check your spelling and keep the letter neat, tidy and easy to read.

If you are trying to get a resolution to a problem, state the problem at the beginning of the letter and if you know how you would like to see the situation resolved, get that message across early on as well. Stick to the points and be as specific as possible with information that will help the recipient fully understand your issues. Note any reference numbers or previous correspondence on business letters to help cut down on the response time. It is always good to set a time frame for the next action and make a note to follow up at that time.

Detail all the ways you have tried to resolve the problem on your own. This is a way of showing your good intentions to work things out and will often result in a more favourable outcome. The responsibility you take by working things out on your own helps you to build the self-confidence you need to effectively get what you want.

Imagine happy outcomes and end the letter as if it has already happened. Try something like 'I know that we will be able to resolve this issue to everyone's highest advantage and look forward to hearing from you', inserting your time frame to work towards resolution. Whereas with personal contact – either in person or by phone – you have an idea of the outcome, a letter leaves you hanging in the air. Once you post the letter, let it go joyously and give it no more thought. By expecting things to work out the best for all, you will find that in the end it works out the way it is intended.

Highly interactive – Immediate time frame – Unclear outcome

E-mail/text

I must confess from the outset that I love the immediacy of text messages and emails to communicate a short and sweet message and I delight even more in receiving them back and knowing that in a spare moment, someone may be thinking about me! And because it is such an easy thing to do from almost anywhere in the world, it is more tempting still to be able to share things so quickly over great distances. I remember when I got a text message from a friend as she was standing on The Great Wall of China to tell me that people were discussing my television series rather than looking at the view. I was completely overwhelmed!

There is also a magical element to the process of seeing your words disappear off into the ether and a bit of excitement in knowing that someone is sharing your words instantly. I have many single friends of both sexes who constantly use texts to flirt and say things they would never dream of saying in person. The anonymity and immediacy of the medium allows you to do things on the spur of the moment and test the waters for a reaction to avoid the embarrassment of saying it face to face. Although it may be fun and exciting in the initial stages of a potential romance, life is not reduced to sound bites, and direct personal contact is the best way to more fully get to the heart of the matter.

The advent of sophisticated wireless technology has enabled even young children to express their thoughts to anyone at any time in most parts of the world. It doesn't matter what time it is at the other end, as the message will be there waiting. Because it is such an instantaneous medium, we expect and often get instantaneous responses to our messages, meaning that there is often little time and thought put into the answer.

Texts and emails can also be a way of avoiding an issue. The on-the-go nature of mobile phones implies that you are too busy to call. There are many occasions, such as cancelling an event or delivering bad news, that should never be done via abbreviated messages. It is only by acknowledging your actions that you can feel happiest in yourself.

By all means use these amazing technologies to get and receive information, but think before you click.

When to speak up

It is not always appropriate to say what is on your mind, no matter how difficult it may be to control the temptation. As you grew up, you learned many rules; among them were guidelines for how to behave in social or public situations. Your earliest lessons probably involved learning to say something nice when you first see someone, and that is still the best way to start any conversation. You may also have been taught that if you can't find something nice to say, don't say anything at all – another good lesson that will stand the test of time. On some occasions, you might even have been taught it is necessary to tell a social fib – such as pretending to like food you are being served.

Social situations differ from other situations, as they are one-off occasions that may differ from one time to the next. The simple fact that you don't have to do it on a daily basis often means that you can find it easy to accept for a short duration of time, even if you do not like it. We often make some sacrifices for those we love, or to advance our careers. The most beneficial way to enter into that sort of situation is to play a little game – sort of like I Spy – and look for every good thing you can find. It takes your mind away from what you may really be thinking and wanting to say, and it makes you and everyone around you feel amazingly better in the process.

While it may not be appropriate to react or speak out in the moment if it would hurt someone's feelings or not solve the problem, there are ways that you can work around the situation for the future. The next time you are invited to dinner, you may tell your hosts what foods you don't eat. It avoids embarrassment and allows you to show your preferences. If you have to visit someone you find boring, find a stimulating activity that you can do together to have something new to talk about. There are many ways that you can still have your voice, although perhaps not in such a direct manner.

Routine situations

The times you are most likely to voice your opinion are in the areas that impact your life on a daily basis. Personal and work relationships, and the associated activities surrounding them, take up all of your waking hours, so you are bound to have developed preferences about your likes and dislikes. The sooner you are able to verbalize and address things that you don't like in any of the situations you face, the less time you will spend doing it. It is also less likely that it will turn into emotional resentment. Developing an honest and open rapport with those around you will allow you to feel confident that things are generally going well. When you have a continuous dialogue, you always know where you stand. As soon as you merely speculate about what other people are thinking, rather than communicating directly, you waste a lot of time and feel bad in the process.

If you find it difficult to state your preferences, start with the least emotional things that you have to decide upon. Look at some of the easy ways to get used to voicing your opinion on a daily basis. Tell the relevant person what you want in the following situations for the next few days and be sure to clearly communicate your desires verbally to the appropriate person in each situation.

- What time would you like to eat your meals, or go to sleep?
- Where would you like to go for lunch?

- Who would you like to talk to, or see, in the course of the day?
- What do you want to do to relax in the evening?

The more you are able to state your preferences, the more likely you are to be understood for the person that you are, giving you the confidence to make your unique contribution in each situation. As you get more comfortable with stating your simple preferences, begin to incorporate your more emotional preferences to those around you.

> *I would really like to do more of . . . in my job/personal life.*
> *I would really like to spend more time with . . .*
> *I would really like to earn more money; is there anything I can do to work towards a promotion?*
> *I would really like to have a tidy house. How can we achieve it?*

When you say these out loud, see how they feel! By stating your preferences in a positive way, you are asking for what you want, rather than discussing what you don't have – a huge difference in how you feel and how the receiver feels about the information. It is impossible for anyone to disagree with any of these statements or questions, because you are only stating what *you* want!

When you encounter a situation that you want to address immediately, look at the following guidelines to steer clear of misunderstandings.

- Is it something that happens often?
- Do you think it is as a result of carelessness or thoughtlessness?
- Do you think it was intentional?

- How does it make you feel?
- How does it affect your ability to perform in or enjoy the situation?

Before you address any issue, take a few minutes to assess the situation. If upon reflection you believe the situation is unintentional and happens on only rare occasions, you may want to let the situation pass and think about a positive way you can address it at a time when you are less emotional about it.

If it is something that happens quite frequently, again, in most cases it is more from a lack of awareness than intent that people do things that may not be to your preference, so to address the issue, wait for the emotions to subside, and state your preferences rather than pointing the finger of blame.

Let's take the example of a communal kitchen – either at home or in the workplace.

If one person occasionally forgets to put something away, and on one occasion you spot them leaving the area without tidying up, at that moment, you may have the impulse to speak out. If you do it in the moment, your emotions may get the better of you and you may react immediately in a negative way. By taking the time to assess the situation, you may realize that you have rarely seen this person make a mess before, so it doesn't really help to say something as it is not significant enough. However, if you always see the person neglecting to tidy up and you want the person to become aware of how their behaviour affects you, you could easily say, 'I really enjoy coming into a clean dining room to eat my lunch. Would you mind helping out?' Rather than finding fault, which immediately creates resistance to the situation, you enlist help in achieving what you want without making the other person feel bad. It works every time!

Delivering the message

Every situation that you face causes you to react in a different manner and your tone, volume and intensity of voice will reflect the changes in your emotional attitude. If you are frightened you may scream; if you are angry you may shout; if you are delivering words of love, you may whisper them in someone's ear; and if you are sad, your voice may seem low to the ground. Within an instant of hearing the voice of the people you know well or love, you can judge their mood.

Say the following phrases out loud and see how they make you feel:

> *I love you.*
> *I hate you.*
> *I am excited about . . .*
> *I am worried about . . .*
> *I am content.*
> *I am angry.*
> *I desire . . .*
> *I am jealous of . . .*
> *I can . . .*
> *I won't . . .*

I'm sure that you can easily feel the difference in how your emotions/feelings impact not only on how you feel, but also on how your voice sounds. If you always deliver your message by first bringing yourself to a place in your mind where you can feel the positive energy of wanting to move forward, you will be able to get your message across in the best manner possible.

The following behaviours show your intent to resolve the

situation to everyone's satisfaction and to create the least resistance to your words.

- Always arrive on time. If you have to be late, call in advance.
- Always start with a smile on your face to set the tone of the conversation.
- Always say thank you for being allowed the opportunity to speak.
- Always make eye contact.
- Always speak from first-hand knowledge.
- Always start with the positive side of the issue.
- Always let people complete their thoughts and don't cast judgement on their opinions.
- Always try to see things from the other person's perspective.
- Always look for common ground.
- Sit comfortably and avoid crossing your arms or your legs in an exaggerated manner.
- Dress for success.
- Turn off mobile phones.
- Schedule enough time to potentially resolve the problem.
- Always say thank you at the end of the conversation for being allowed to say all that you have said, and reaffirm that you have the highest intentions.

When your voice is not heard

Sometimes, it is easy to get the timing wrong when trying to express your thoughts. You might have put your message across in a way that the person could not understand, or the person might not have been capable of accepting the information at that point in time. We are all on our individual paths – sometimes they meet, sometimes they unite and upon occasion they collide.

If you have been unsuccessful at achieving a result that you desire, it's always good to meditate on the situation and address it in another place or time that feels right. By meditating on the issue, you let it go and revisit it with a fresh outlook when the situation presents itself again. Letting go of the emotional attachments of your past experiences enables you to see things that you were not able to clearly see before.

If you find that you feel strongly about a situation that you are unable to change to your satisfaction, and the situation makes you feel bad and occupies your thoughts, it becomes a liability to hold it inside. You must consciously choose a way forward that helps to resolve the situation, if only by deciding that it isn't a 'deal-breaker' – in other words, it is not your last stand or opinion on the matter.

To progress in a positive manner towards harmonious resolution, you have three options:

Same

Expressing your opinion has not resolved the situation. Your first approach did not work and you may decide that although it is important to you, the positives of the situation outweigh the negatives and you accept that the situation stays the same.

To progress forward, you take your mind away from the thing that upsets you or that has not been resolved, and actively choose to do positive things that make *you* feel better. Remember, it can be anything that is good for you and brings you pleasure that can dramatically alter your feelings in the moment. If you continue to ignore the negatives, you will soon not notice them and they will seem very insignificant.

Compromise

If you can't remove your mind from the situation, go for a compromise. If you are willing to move towards the centre and offer this openly, it makes it easier for the other person to respond. By stating that you can see the other person's point of view and want to come to a common ground, it is a win–win situation. Everyone feels that they have done the right thing and you can find peace of mind.

Don't be disheartened if the first negotiations don't work out as you would like. There are many issues of ego and control built into every type of relationship that often occur in times of dissention. It is important to remember that even a small step forward in a positive direction, feels far better than no movement at all.

Leave

At some time in your life you may feel so strongly about your beliefs or opinions in a situation, that even with your best intentions, your views and those of the people involved in the area of conflict just do not mesh. You are unable to find a way to compromise on a happy resolution for all involved, and you don't feel the situation enhances your growth and development. This is a juncture where you have an opportunity for great growth, where you are able to put your own interests ahead of others and choose to do something that is more in line with your current way of thinking. It happens. People leave jobs, get divorced, choose different friends, change careers and make choices on a daily basis according to their feelings and principles. How many times have you left a queue when there were too many people in line?

It is never, ever easy to leave a situation where there are feelings involved. It is very easy to feel guilty about being selfish over things that are very important to you, and letting people down, but in the end, you really must always take the decision based on what makes you feel good. Without that, you and those around you will be miserable as a result, and in the long run, it can adversely affect your health.

No matter how unhappy you may be in your current situation, when the time comes to part company, let me offer these words of advice:

- Always look at the positive things the experience has taught you.
- Always end on a happy note – thank them for contributing to your life.
- Always leave the door open – you have many things in common and will meet again.
- Always express your thoughts in person.
- Never point out the negative things unless asked. Then do it in a loving and gentle manner.
- Always take responsibility for your decision. Do things because you want to do them rather than as a response to someone's actions. It puts the onus on the wants and desires that you want to have fulfilled.
- Always let out your emotions about the situation at an appropriate time. The sooner you are able to express your thoughts verbally to others, the fewer burdens you will feel about your decision. Once you say something out loud in the presence of someone else, it affirms your intention. If you can look at the

positive ways you are planning to make changes for the better, you will leave the negative feelings behind in little time.

To many, your words mean more than you think

It is truly difficult to understand the impact that you may have on people and how much they may value your opinion. Three simple words like 'I love you' can change someone's life, or day, or minute. Even telling a complete stranger that they look great can tremendously change the fate of two people's lives. Once you have a positive experience, it lifts your spirits and helps you to continue seeing things in a positive frame of mind for longer than you would have.

You know what it feels like to receive a compliment – it is a wonderful feeling of pride and acceptance of some level of your being. If you tell someone how intelligent he or she is, it helps them to gain confidence in their way of thinking. If you give someone a compliment about their physical appearance, they will feel fantastic and become aware of what it was on the day that made them look so well. If you tell your partner they are a wonderful lover – ooh la la! Each time you pay someone a compliment, you help to bolster their self-confidence and show them you appreciate their actions.

This is how it works.

When you pay a compliment, you are looking at the best the situation has to offer. It makes you feel good. It makes the recipient feel even better!

We have looked at how your habits impact those around you. One of the effects of a habit is that you remove your awareness from the situation. In developing habits at work and at home it is easy to take for granted the routine actions of your partner/family/colleagues or people who help you out with their services, like babysitters, cleaners, or anyone who improves the quality of your day.

By getting into the habit of starting each new part of your day looking at what uplifts your spirit in the situation, you will find it easy to spread the feeling throughout the day and to those around you.

- Say something nice first thing in the morning to the one closest to you.
- Look for something to say on your way to work/ shopping or during the first activity of the day. I always tell the staff at my local coffee shop how they make my day bright and early in the morning. They always know what I want before I get into the door because I show my appreciation by paying a compliment.
- Look for something uplifting to say to people you care about in your work environment. Try it on everyone in one day and see what your vibe is around the office.
- Pay a compliment to someone or about something you see outside. It could be a neighbour's flowers or pet, or a new butcher in the neighbourhood. Showing that you are aware of how their contribution makes your life more stimulating makes for new friendships or feelings of goodwill.
- At the end of the day, pay the biggest compliment to yourself, for all of the positive things you have enjoyed and accomplished in the course of the day.

Positive affirmations

According to the dictionary, 'to affirm' means that you declare positively or firmly a belief that you maintain to be true. When you make an affirmation out loud, the universe witnesses your intention and belief. The more you are able to use your voice to positively remind yourself of all of the wonderful, natural, joyful aspects of your character, the more you will allow them to be heard through your actions and deeds.

Find yourself a quiet and comfortable spot at the end of the day and spend a few minutes affirming your voice to the universe. If you practise a faith, it is a good time to talk to your higher source of inspiration.

> *I am a loving person. Today I shared my love with . . .*
> *I am a thoughtful person. Today I thought about . . .*
> *I am a kind person. Today I was kind to . . .*
> *I am a generous person. Today I shared with . . .*
> *I am a healthy person. Today I looked after my body by . . .*
> *I am a wise person. Today I learned . . .*
> *I am an adaptable person. Today I experienced these new things . . .*
> *I am a good listener. Today I really listened to . . .*
> *I am an honest person. Today I gave the following things all of my effort . . .*

If you practise these affirmations on a nightly basis for a few weeks, you will begin to see the difference in how you feel about yourself. You will feel more confident that you are worthy of having an opinion that matters, and you will allow more of the person that you know is on the inside to be seen on the outside, and allow yourself to shine through.

The dos and don'ts of speaking up

Listen first, speak last

When I was a child, my mother taught me this nursery rhyme:

> *A wise old owl sat on an oak,*
> *The more he heard, the less he spoke.*
> *The less he spoke, the more he heard.*
> *Why aren't we all like that wise old bird?*

Give yourself time to process the information you hear before you offer an opinion. It helps to formulate your thoughts, keeping in mind the most current information that can help you to adapt your opinions to the current situation.

Speak from your heart

If you always have the highest intentions for the positive outcome of a conversation, you will find the easiest and best ways to convey your message. Speaking from your heart does not imply that the conversation has to be an emotional one; just one that is right for you to have at the time.

Never speak behind someone's back

Always go to the source to get the story straight. We are all guilty of having a gossip about people and things that are going on around us. It is a way of sharing information about what other people perceive is going on in situations that you have in common. Unfortunately, it is also the easiest way to misunderstanding any situation, as by taking other people's perceptions as fact, you formulate your opinions based on hearsay. If you can speak about other people, you can also imagine that they are speaking about you!

Don't speak out in anger

There are no occasions when speaking out in anger makes you feel good, but in cases of extreme danger, such as witnessing a crime or seeing someone physically harm another, your emotions go into overdrive and you react without thinking. Although reason may also prevail in such a situation, the immediacy of the danger kicks your adrenaline into action and you are often unaware of your actions.

In any situation other than an emergency, anger never solves a problem. It can allow your voice to be heard, but the extreme reaction makes the gap really wide before you can come to an agreement. Another old childhood adage, 'Count to 10 when you are angry,' gives you a better chance to gain perspective and come from a moderated position, bringing resolution much closer. It feels better physically, as well!

Healthy arguments, however, can help to clear the air and allow your voice to be heard. To argue constructively, remove the emotion from the situation and try to be logical in your approach. It also helps to keep the tone of your voice at a moderate level. It is as important to listen as it is to speak, as it is through listening to others' points of view that you expand your mind and gain perspective.

Don't speak out of turn

A friend of mine recently went to a strategy session with a group of people who were unknown to each other. There were two rules laid out on the table before the session began.

1 No one was allowed to comment on another's opinion.
2 Everyone would go around the room in turn and answer the same question from their own perspective.

For her, it was one of the most productive and interesting sessions she had attended. No one was threatened because his or her ideas, like everyone else's ideas, were brought forward and looked at equally. Everyone was guaranteed the opportunity to speak in a non-hostile environment. It was a brilliant strategy to make for the most creative solutions.

When you show your intention to participate in a mutually beneficial conversation to positively move forward, you take into account everyone's point of view. By waiting your turn, you acknowledge everyone else's contribution to making the thing work.

Don't hog the limelight

No matter how riveting a personality you think you have, you'll never learn anything new by always being the centre of attention. Although it may feel good to have your moment in the spotlight, and it does feel good, let others share the same experience. Everyone has their own unique story to bring to any occasion and they deserve their chance to shine.

7.

In the Grand Scale of Life

Everyday, you react to experiences according to how they affect you in the moment. If you take a sip out of a cup of scalding coffee and you burn your tongue, you might get cross or even yell out in pain. As the pain subsides, you gradually forget about the experience. Although it might make you more cautious next time you take a sip of coffee, the overall impact of this unpleasant experience, *in the moment*, won't have long-lasting effects on your life.

However, sometimes, we have an experience that may be unpleasant in the moment, like missing a train for work when you have an important meeting, and this single experience can be something that we think about for days, weeks and even months! *A single experience can consume all of your thoughts and play a disproportionate part in your life.* Until you are able to gain some perspective, you are likely to be in for an emotional and rocky road ahead.

Learning to put things into perspective will save you, and those around you, a lot of time, energy and worry. If, rather than reacting in an emotional way and looking at how you may be affected in the moment, you are able to see how this one event compares to the really important things to you in your life, you can easily see that it really doesn't matter very much. To keep things in perspective in any situation, ask yourself the following questions:

- What is the significance of this event in my life?
- Is this something that can be resolved? If so, what can I do to resolve this on my own?
- Is this something that will matter in a week?
- Is this something that will have long-term effects on my life?

In just the short time that it may take you to answer these questions, you can distance yourself enough from how the situation feels the second it happens, in order to make more informed decisions about how to react.

> Several years ago, I got a phone call from a family member whose first panicked words were, 'There's been a disaster!' Now these words put me into serious alert mode, knowing that certain members of the family were seriously ill. I braced myself for the worst news possible, only to be told that the refrigerator had broken down, or she had forgotten to pay an outstanding bill. To tell you the truth, I can't even remember what the momentary crisis may have been.

Was this in fact a disaster, or a minor inconvenience that could be easily solved? When you look at the broader perspective of real and true disasters where innocent lives are lost, then in the grand scale of life, this doesn't mean very much. Although it may have been an unpleasant experience in the moment, will you even remember it next week?

Let's face it; if you had to list the 10 most important things in your life, I'm sure that neither the bill nor the refrigerator would qualify for the top 1000 or even 10,000, never mind the top 10. In other words, some things justify more of your thoughts and have greater impact on your life than others. To put things into perspective, you need to step back from the situation and look at it in relation to others. When you look at the perspective of a drawing, you see the size of one object relative to another object and this gives you the understanding of where everything fits into the picture. The same is true with life. When you judge things based on a broader viewpoint, you are able to see more of the picture.

I had another experience just yesterday when I was doing a live radio programme, talking about the benefits of de-cluttering your possessions. It was one of the few interviews that I have given over many years where the broadcaster did not believe it was a good idea to get rid of things you no longer use. Trying to get to the root of the problem, I asked if there was a specific incident that had happened in his life to make him feel so strongly on the subject. He relayed in detail an incident where his mother had thrown out a collection of toys without asking and now they would be quite valuable. I probed a bit further and found out that he was in his fifties, and that his mother had passed away over 25 years ago, and he still held this resentment over children's toys.

My advice was to get some perspective! I told him that at the end of his life, which I hope is a long way off, did he think that this one incident would really matter? Would he remember the material possessions, or all the people and wonderful experiences he had in his life? I asked him to listen to the broadcast again to hear how much anger he had held on to for so many years. I don't know whether my words had an impact, but when you are able to step back and see what really matters to your happiness, you will find that you probably already have what really counts.

What's important in the grand scale of your life?

Throughout the book we have looked at how many of your past experiences have contributed to your current perspective. We have looked at ways of becoming aware of habits that require more attention, of letting go of old experiences that keep you stuck in the past and ways of developing a positive mental attitude, and the many methods you can put in place that will help you to more easily moderate your reactions to the stresses and strains of daily living.

Half the battle is to look at things with the most positive outlook you can muster and the other half is to judge things on the relative scale of how they will affect your overall health, wealth and happiness, not in the moment, but in a week's time, a month's time or at some time in the future. Taken to a higher degree, look at how your issues compare with those less fortunate people in the world – this is a quick way to bring you back to a greater sense of perspective.

Every day you work hard to accomplish the targets you set yourself. Some days you cross everything off your list, other days you barely make a dent, but in the grand scale of life, it's not getting the dishes done or finishing up a project that really matters. It's the time you spend being happy, playing with your children, canoodling with your loved one, seeing the grandchildren, eating a meal with friends, going on holiday, reading a book to expand your mind; the list goes on and on. We don't live our lives to achieve; we achieve to live our lives. In trying to do the achieving, we often find it very easy to forget about the living. Back to my favourite line – we're here for a good time, not a long time, so make every minute count doing the things that make you feel good.

It's really easy to get things out of perspective when you forget the things that really, really matter to you in your life.

Whatever you imagine is at the end of your career rainbow, I am sure that you imagine yourself relaxed, happy, in good physical condition, and surrounded by people you love. You may picture yourself in a different part of the country or the world, in a different house with more money and more things, but basically, your ultimate goal in your life is to be healthy, happy and able to do what you want. I bet if you took the time to think about it, you would find that most of the things you want out of your lifetime, you already have.

On a daily basis, there are very few things that can impact on your ability to achieve these things, because you have complete control over how you feel on every level and you always have the choice to do what makes you happy. You know how to maintain your physical health by watching what you eat and staying fit. You know the things that make you happy. Most importantly, you can always choose how to react in every situation to achieve your desired result of feeling good. So when a day goes by and you aren't able to finish things, or you miss a train or the refrigerator breaks down, you know that they cannot impact on the grand scale, so why put yourself through the unpleasantness.

To help you maintain perspective over the little, unimport-ant events in your life, make a list of the 10 intangible things that you have that are most important to you. These are things you will always have, regardless of whatever circum-stances come your way.

What's your take on life?

I sincerely believe that we all have the ability to shift our general outlook in life towards believing that it is possible to have happy outcomes in all that we do. This is an optimistic perspective, meaning you go into each situation looking for the best ways to achieve your desired result. If you are optimistic, you generally feel happy and upbeat most of the time because that is what you are focusing your attention on. Even in an unpleasant situation, your optimistic nature allows you to look beyond what you see in the present to a future point where you believe that things will be better. Optimism owes a lot to confidence and faith.

Your overall perspective is how you view life, generally. You know the classic question, 'Do you see the glass as half full or half empty?' If you see it half full, your nature is optimistic and you don't let past negative experiences weigh you down. You believe that good things often happen and will continue to happen regardless of the experiences you have in the moment. You have developed a positive mental attitude and know that tomorrow is another day to begin again. In most new experiences you will look for positive ways to deal with them.

If you see the glass as half empty, you are more pessimistic by nature. You let negative experiences of the past influence your future and you often look at the worst in a situation. You may worry about not having enough or think that each new situation is bad until proven good. It doesn't often feel very good to be pessimistic. You see the worst in each experience unnecessarily. You may also spend a lot of time hypothesizing about what negative things may happen in the future so that you rarely see or experience the more pleasant aspects of life.

Although you may be generally one way or the other, you

may be a combination – optimistic about some areas and pessimistic about others. The areas that you feel optimistic about probably run quite smoothly, as you are anticipating the best in each situation. The pessimistic areas are probably as a result of negative experiences you have had in the past that you allow to influence your new experiences. If you think that something will turn out badly, you can easily find something negative to focus on. Unless it is your job to always look at the downside, as a general rule of life it won't get you where you want to be.

Your general outlook in each of these areas will determine how you are predisposed to looking at each new experience in this area. Take a look and see what your general feelings are about each of the following areas:

	Optimistic	Unsure	Pessimistic
Health			
Personal relationships			
Family			
Professional life			
Financial security			
Trying new things			
Reaching your goals			
Achieving happiness			
Intelligence			
Ability to handle crisis			

I hope that you find many areas of your life where you have an optimistic outlook. You will find that these areas make you feel good and confident and able to make decisions based on the anticipation of a happy outcome. The more you are able to anticipate a positive result, the more often you get one.

In the areas where you are more pessimistic, you probably don't give it all of your effort, as you don't believe the situation will end well. If you have had a rocky love life, you may be pessimistic about dating or getting involved with someone in the future. In each new relationship, you may look at all the negatives, which in the long run will make it impossible for you to find someone suitable. If your partner passed away you may believe that you will never find anyone as good in the future, and with this attitude, you are unlikely to ever put yourself in the position of meeting new people.

It is good to look at the reasons behind your pessimism. Is it fact or fiction? Many things that you worry about have no basis or foundation, other than your assumptions, and often these are not based on reality. In these situations, it is good to seek another opinion. The objective opinion of a professional or someone you trust can help you to see things from a basis of fact. A good case may be if you worry unnecessarily about money. If you can see a report in black and white, issued by an objective source, it can help you to change your perspective. If you think you can't do something and never try, how do you ever know whether you can do it?

Try this exercise to shift your view from can't to can do.

- Write down the area of your life where you are most pessimistic.
- Write down as many things as possible to make you more optimistic about a situation. Then spend another 5 minutes thinking about even the tiniest things that would make you feel more optimistic, and write them down.

- Number them, starting with the easiest thing that you can do to feel more optimistic.
- Each day, concentrate on one new optimistic way of looking at the situation.
- If you practise this daily, you will certainly feel better and you will shift your attitude without even realizing it.

How we see things

When you interpret an experience based on how it makes you feel, your perspective on the experience is subjective, meaning that it cannot be verified or proven because it is not based on facts, but on how you feel about what has happened. Each person experiencing the same situation will have a different perspective. You have experienced this at social gatherings or even in work situations where you have all been to the same event and your view and that of the others differed. Your opinion is subjective – how the event influenced you. When you listen to everyone's view, you gain a broader perspective on what has happened.

An objective point of view means that you remove your personal feelings about the situation, and look at it uninfluenced by your personal prejudices. An objective point of view removes the emotional elements from your judgement and allows you to see things in a different light. You may get an objective point of view from a professional you seek assistance from – a doctor, a lawyer or an accountant – who tells you the straightforward facts. It is easier to have an objective point of view about things that do not directly affect you; however there are many ways to become more objective and less reactive in most situations that you experience in your life.

Sometimes you may have a very narrow point of view about something, meaning that you are unwilling to expand your perspective on that matter. If you decide that you are going shopping for a white shirt and that is all you are willing to look at, that is a narrow perspective. You are focused on one thing and unwilling to be swayed by any other influence.

You may also have a narrow perspective on politics or world matters, religion or anything else that impacts on your life, and these are the areas where a broader perspective may be beneficial. It is only by comparing your views with others' views that you know whether there is something that would make you think or act in a new way. The more open-minded you are, the more you will expand and find solutions to problems or new experiences that will make your life more stimulating.

- Do you ever change your mind about the kinds of food you eat?
- Do you ever change your mind about the styles of clothing you wear?
- Do you ever change your view of what is happening in the world?
- Do you ever change your mind about people you know?
- Do you ever change your mind about something you intended to do in the course of the day?

Let's look at an example of a subjective, an objective and a narrow point of view.

If I asked you to *exactly describe* an object in the window of a department store, you would probably talk about its size, shape, colour or texture and anything else that is distinguishing about it. The way that you describe it would probably be quite similar to the way someone else describes it with a few minor variations. This would be an *objective* viewpoint because you are describing exactly what you see without emotional input.

Now, if I asked you what you *thought* about an object in the window of a department store, you would look at the item and compare it to other similar items that you have known in your life and describe your preferences. You might like what it can be used for, or how it will work within the confines of your home. This description now has your personal viewpoint attached to it, and it will most certainly differ from the viewpoints of other people, as they have had different experiences. What you think about something is your *subjective* view.

Someone with a narrow point of view probably wouldn't undertake the description in the first place. If it didn't fit into something that they already had in mind, they would be too dismissive and unwilling to try even describing something new.

When a subjective viewpoint works to your benefit:

- Expressing opinions on subjects you are passionate about such as art or music
- Determining your personal priorities for the day
- Taking personal decisions.

When an objective viewpoint works to your benefit:

- Taking decisions that affect others
- Solving problems
- Giving useful advice
- De-personalizing situations

● Assessing situations
● Dealing with family matters.

When a narrow viewpoint works to your benefit:

● Working to accomplish a single goal.

I would say that a narrow viewpoint is rarely beneficial as it limits the possibility that something new can change your viewpoint! In the case of the white shirt, perhaps blue, pink or yellow would have been better!

How we gain perspective

You put things into perspective as a result of your general outlook on life, the experiences you have had to date, and your age. Other people's input can also give you a change of perspective, and so can the passage of time, as you gain more experiences that can help you to put behind you the older, less pleasant memories. Until you take an active part in gaining perspective, you can spend a good deal of your life leading a very unhappy existence by letting the little things ruin the precious time that you have on this earth. Whenever life takes you by surprise, you need to find the best way to keep things in perspective.

The one way that we all gain perspective is through the passage of time. Whatever was the most important thing in your life when you were 8 will surely not be the most important thing at 13 or 27 or 83, because over time and, with the benefit of experience, the relative importance of events in your life changes.

Where you are on your life's path alters your perspective on the relative importance of the events in your life.

Look at how your perspective may change as a result of your age:

0–12

When you were a child with limited experiences, each individual event held a lot of importance to you as you had limited perspective. The child next door got a new toy and his friend got a new toy and you wanted a new toy, because in your limited exposure, everyone around you was getting a new toy.

Teens

As you entered your teens, you spread your wings and experienced lots and lots of new things. Each new event was important in the moment, but you were so busy thinking about the next new experience that the relative importance of each one probably became less significant. You may have been madly in love with one person, had your heart broken, then in a few weeks' time you found yourself wildly in love with someone else.

20s

As you get into your twenties, you probably feel more pressure to take bigger life decisions to begin to shape your future. Your perspective in this stage of your life may be that the decisions you make have more importance, as you are beginning to view how you would like your future to be and know that you need to work to get there. At this stage of life it is easy to worry so much about the decision, that you miss many opportunities along the way.

30s

As you enter your thirties, you start feeling the effects of time pressures, such as your biological clock, or making sure that your career advances on track to achieve your goals. You look at what you had hoped to achieve and can often look at the things that you don't have rather than what you do, and feel under pressure to reach your desired goals before time runs out. Some areas may be out of balance as a result of your quest to fulfil other areas, and this can cause you to get things out of perspective.

40s and 50s

Many people experience a mid-life crisis, during which they question their values and perspective. This is usually prompted by a series of events – job change, kids leaving home, grey hairs, the death of a loved one or whatever it is that points out the passing of time. This is a time of your life when you can have a huge shift in perspective. You may make radical choices to achieve the happiness that you have worked for.

60s and 70s

Most people hope to achieve retirement by this age, if not sooner. At this point in your life, you may feel and see the physical effects of time on your body. If your general out-look on life is a positive one, you will still have a healthy perspective on the prospects for the remainder of your life. Your brain does not stop producing brain cells, regardless of your age. It is the lack of desire that stops your mind dead in its tracks. I believe that a healthy perspective not only helps you to enjoy your life to the fullest, it also helps to extend your life.

If you are cynical, your perspective may be one of looking at all the things you have lost – most frequently health, youth, people of significance in your life, or a career that you spent many years developing. You may feel displaced by the lack of activities in your life. This stops the flow of desire for you to continue to experience new things. It also makes many of the things that you do experience more unpleasant than need be.

Do you see the glass half empty or half full?

80+

With medical technology extending the average life expectancy by years over previous generations, you can still have a great, active life for as long as you continue to summon the energy to do and try new things. Your perspective when you reach this age in your life is critical to maintaining your mental and physical health. If at any time you give up the will to continue, or stop doing the daily things that help to keep your mind fit, you can begin to decline way before your time. The quality of your life can dictate your perspective on your future.

Now take a look at how your perspective on life has changed over the last few years:

- Are the same things that were important to you a year ago still as important now?
- What about 5 years ago?
- What things, if any, have made you change your perspective?

Even a short period of time can change your perspective

The examples listed above look at the broader perspective of time. However, it is easy to gain some perspective even with a short passage of time. Any distance of time that you place between a situation and your reaction to it will enable you to get a broader perspective. As little as 5 minutes can allow you to look at things more objectively.

Let's take an example – you lose your handbag and in the moment you absolutely panic and think it is the worst thing that could possibly happen. You assume that it has been stolen, or lost forever, and worry about your cash, your credit cards and the hassle that it will take to get them all again. You go into a panic mode that makes you feel awful on every level. You spend so much time flapping about, that you make no progress in solving the problem.

If you were able to step back from the situation and look at it as an observer, with objectivity, you would first take the necessary time to think about all the places that you had been during the day. You would try to remember the last place you had it. You would then take action and retrace your steps to find it. This gives you a better chance of solving the problem and you will feel a whole lot better in the process. Taking even a small amount of time is better than taking no time before you react to a problem.

Take a look at the events in the last 30 days of your life and see what might have been improved if you had given the matter more time before reacting:

- What made you lose your temper?
- What upset you?
- What couldn't you figure out?
- Is there anything that you thought was more important than it turned out to be?
- Did you say anything that you hadn't thought about?
- What have you changed your mind about? What caused you to change your mind?

Other people's opinions can change your perspective

One of the best ways to broaden your perspective is to take into account others' views on the matter. You can do this by talking to friends or experts, doing some research or deciding to further your education relative to the area where you need to gain perspective. From the first time that you were influenced by someone other than your parents, you started to broaden your perspective by trying and learning new things. Your studies opened your mind to new possibilities that you may not have otherwise experienced. You have been able to benefit from other people's experiences, and know that even if they have not existed for you, they can exist. Being open-minded means just that – you are open to all the possibilities that exist, whether you have experienced them or not. It doesn't rule out any possibilities, no matter how unrealistic you may feel they are in the moment.

Whenever your emotions are involved in a situation, you probably do not see the full picture or the overall relevance of the event in your life. We have all been wrapped up in our emotions and unable to get a clear picture of how to move forward in the best way possible. A simple example can be deciding what to wear on a big night out. You really, really want to look fantastic to feel good about yourself and perhaps you even want to impress someone else. You get so wound up about how you look that you find it difficult to get perspective about what looks the best. A great way to overcome this is to get an objective opinion from someone who is not emotionally involved in the situation and whose opinion you trust. You can gain confidence by getting another point of view.

List the people you know whose opinions you trust on the following matters:

- Your health
- Your love life
- Your financial security
- Your house
- Professional decisions
- Your children
- Your future
- Legal matters

Never be afraid to ask for help. People are flattered when you seek their opinion. Whenever you ask for help, you show an intention to solve the problem. One of my greatest tools for sorting out problems over the phone with nameless, faceless people is to explain my situation and ask them what they would do if they were me. It immediately changes their perspective to a more empathetic position, rather than taking the company line. It always works to get the problem solved. Draw upon your list of helpful people to give you some solutions that you could not see from your own perspective.

If you find yourself in a position where you cannot get in touch with someone whose opinion you trust, try this very simple exercise to gain a different point of view. For this exercise, it doesn't matter whether the person is living or has passed away, as long as you have trust in what they would tell you.

Sit somewhere quiet, away from the source of conflict. Imagine yourself in a place that you and your trusted friend spent some time together, where they told you meaningful things that have helped you at some time in your life. Think about the issue that you are trying to resolve and ask your friend what they would do. Relax and listen to what they would tell you. Thank them for their words of wisdom and sit quietly for a few minutes as you think about how these words will impact on your situation. Have faith that the answers will be right for you.

Setting priorities – how your perspective impacts on your daily life

Everyday, you compare the value of one thing against another as you decide how to plan your day. You decide what areas of your life are going to get attention, and who you want to see or speak with, and you map out a strategy to get them all done. In other words, you set your priorities for the day based on how important you view each item in the day to be. How you feel at the end of the day is often a result of how well you feel you have achieved your daily goals.

If you are like most people, you make a long list of items that you would like to get done. Sometimes you finish everything on the list, but probably more often than not, something unexpected happens or you just run out of time and don't get everything done. At the end of the day, if you judge your achievements based on how much you got done, you can often feel bad about yourself for not reaching your goals. You start the next day carrying the burdens of the previous day, and before you know it, your attitude when you begin each day is so weighted down by thoughts of what you need to do that it is difficult to concentrate on any one thing at a time. Setting unrealistic goals for yourself lowers your self-confidence and sets you up for failure.

In reality, you can never get everything done! There will always be something else to do in the next minute, hour or day, so rushing through life in order to get everything done is self-defeating. You are setting yourself up for an impossible task that feels awful in the process. You get stressed, lose your focus on what you are doing, and end up not getting anything done at all. It is far better to do one thing well and enjoy doing it, than to rush through ten things on your list.

When you need to do something, you worry about the consequences of not getting it done. Would the world come to an end, in reality, if you didn't get it done today but tomorrow instead? It is the very pressure that you place on yourself to complete things that defeats the purpose of what you are trying to achieve, which is to feel good and enjoy the experience. Each day you work towards an end, but isn't the end to relax, have fun and enjoy all the things you have and do? Can you do that if you worry about all the things you don't have or haven't done?

To get an idea of what you may feel an obligation to do, as opposed to what you may want to do, see how the following routine tasks make you feel:

- Going grocery shopping
- Going shopping for a new outfit
- Preparing a meal for yourself
- Preparing a meal for close friends
- Having to pick up your children from school
- Reading your children a bedtime story
- Wanting to do your best on a project
- Having to complete a project in an hour
- Changing the bed linen
- Getting into a freshly made bed.

Look at the items on the list that you feel *obliged* to do, and for each item, write down five reasons why you *want* to do each thing. For example, you may hate grocery shopping, but when you look at what you want out of the experience, it becomes a different matter. If you look at all the delicious foods you can buy and the meals you will enjoy with your family or friends, the act of shopping becomes a desire for something. You have changed your perspective from need to desire, and in the process you can easily see the benefits of getting it done.

In order to achieve perspective and balance in your life, you need to plan each day so that you can feel your best. To do this, you must incorporate all the things that make you happy into your daily routine.

- What is the one thing that will make you feel best about your appearance?
- When will you have your meals to enable you to keep your energy levels at peak performance?
- Who is the one person you would really like to talk to or see?
- What is the one thing you would like to do in your job?
- What is the one thing you could do to make you happy in your home?
- What is the one thing you would like to do to relax and unwind?

Limiting your goals to one achievable thing in each area of your life that would make you feel good gives you a huge incentive to get it done. If you make time for the things that make you feel good, you will feel good about the things you do. At the end of the day, you have achieved your goals if you have made yourself happy, and in my book, that is what it is all about.

8.
Life Matters

We are all faced with challenges throughout our lives which present us with tremendous opportunities for growth. At some time in your life you will have to accept the loss of a loved one, face personal or professional disappointments, and learn to accept growing older. Each time you face a difficult situation, you have within your power the ability to put things into perspective and look at all the positive ways that you can make the situation the best that it can be. Even in the direst of circumstances, looking for the path forward kick starts your brain into helping you to see the many options ahead. There are always ways in every situation to make you feel better once you make the decision to do so.

During your lifetime, you have probably had a life-changing experience. One moment in time can be enough to transform your life and cause you to look at things completely differently. Life-changing experiences can be a result of very positive things that happen to you such as finding your soul mate, giving birth, accomplishing something you didn't think you could do or winning the lottery – anything that suddenly makes you all of a sudden redefine the importance of the things that you are doing in your life. Life-changing experiences can also be as a result of something that is unpleasant in the moment, such as death, divorce, illness or losing your job; where you question the meaning of your life and the future ahead.

It is in these moments that you begin a new cycle in your

life. In the case of stimulating life-changing moments, it is easy to get excited about the new opportunities that such wonderful experiences bring into your life, as they enable you to dream about a future that feels good. To feel strong in the moments of despair, you must look at what the experience brought to your life. The positive moments can stay with you forever and propel you forward if you can allow your mind to think about them, rather than focusing on all that you think you have lost.

Each experience you have makes you a stronger person, whether it is a good experience or one that you did not find pleasurable, as these experiences help you to more clearly know what you like and want. With unpleasant experiences such as divorce, the death of someone you love or the loss of anything that is important to you, it is because you continue to want to have that same experience that you feel the sense of loss. Once you know the feeling of love, you can love again. Once you know the feeling of working at something you enjoy, you can find that experience again. Once someone has impacted on your life, you can look for the positive ways that they influenced you and carry that with you for evermore. Nothing is ever lost except the time it takes you to realize that life will always go on. It is up to you whether you want to take the big leap forward and start afresh, looking for the next big adventure.

Dealing with disappointments

When something happens that is disappointing, the first thing that most people do is assign blame. They either blame someone else, the circumstances or themselves and none of those choices feels very good. When you assign blame, you hold the negative experience in your mind and it jades your perspective for future experiences. It also keeps you firmly stuck in the past and prevents you from looking for the next opportunity that will come along.

Five years ago I experienced one of my biggest disappointments – I was asked to step down from the position as Managing Director of the company I had founded. For the six previous years I had given my heart and soul to developing the business that was quite well known, but not very profitable. During that time my husband and I put a fair chunk of money into supporting the business and many friends also invested when the company traded its shares on a limited basis.

I was completely devastated and really did feel that I was not treated fairly, yet I did not want to do anything that damaged the reputation of the company that was so closely identified with me. I knew that I did the best possible job that I could have done and that I had nothing to feel ashamed about. Furthermore, I did not want the people who invested in me to lose their investment based on my inability to accept a decision that had been made by a legitimate group.

Everyone around me offered great sympathy and, although greatly appreciated, I hate it when people feel sorry for me. I never made a fuss or spoke badly about anything that had happened, and am pleased that the company continues to trade. Although I have had no involvement in the company since I stepped down, I have always hoped for its continued success – doing anything else would be hurting something that I loved. I moved forward, wrote another book, learned Reiki and, in a very short time, my life was once again transformed. I was asked to be the expert on *The Life Laundry* television series for the BBC and moved from one thing to another without suffering too much in the process.

There is no such thing as failure

No one is perfect at everything, and learning to accept your humanity is often a difficult lesson to take on board. It's not only that you feel you have let yourself down, but it is also the feeling that you have disappointed others that compounds the situation and makes it more difficult to pick yourself up and try again. Expressing your feelings to your loved ones rather than keeping them inside can serve to remind you of how special those around you think you are, regardless of your failings.

Each experience that you have helps you to refine your likes and dislikes. In circumstances where you have not successfully accomplished what you set out to do, you still learned many new things in the process, including defining things that you don't want to do in the same way again. Because you failed at something once, doesn't mean you'll fail at it again. If you have a goal and really want to accomplish it, you will find a better way to achieve it. Like the phoenix that rises from the ashes, from adversity new ideas are born.

We are all human and we do feel bad when things don't go the way we want them to. We want to be loved and respected and to feel that we are good at what we do. It is hard to remove your emotions from a situation when someone rocks your confidence and tells you that you are not good enough. The only thing that can get you beyond that is to know deep down inside that you really are good enough – maybe not perfect, but good enough. If you are always perfect what is there in life that can challenge you?

When you look back at the disappointments you may have faced, I'm certain that you will be able to see that as soon as you let the experience go, something bigger and better came along in its place. I believe that things happen for a reason, and the moment that you are able to see the positive things that you gained from the experience, you will actively de-junk your mind.

Take a look back at things that you thought were disappointing at the time, but later turned out for the best. Think about what happened as a result of not getting what you wanted at that moment.

- Did you meet anyone new?
- Were you presented with different opportunities that turned out better?
- Did you learn new things?
- Did you feel stronger when you finally got over it?

If you still harbour ill feelings, go back to Chapter 3, Forgive and Forget, and work at releasing the experience. Once you do, see how much better it feels in your heart.

Moving on after divorce or break-up

Sometimes in life, even with the best of intentions, things don't work out as you dreamed they would. When it comes to affairs of the heart, the hurt can feel enormous, as you have allowed another person to see inside your soul and share your most intimate feelings. When you are the one left behind, it is easy to feel that you have been betrayed. As in any bereavement, there are many stages you can go through, the most common being shame, anger and depression. If you are the one that is leaving, there are always some feelings of guilt associated with hurting someone you love.

In all probability, the breakdown of your relationship didn't happen overnight. At the beginning of your relationship, you shared common dreams. You might have liked to participate in the same kinds of activities, or shared the same profession, and you looked for all the things that you had in common that you could enjoy together. The longer your relationship continued, the more different types of situations you faced, both personally and as a couple. You took on work responsibilities and household responsibilities and, possibly, raising a family on top of that. It is easy to get so wound up in what you do that you forget to look after yourself and the relationship. It is also easy to feel resentment over trivial things that build up over time.

Whenever you fail to look after yourself, you become less of a person. You don't eat properly, by either under- or overeating, you stop paying attention to your appearance and, most importantly, you stop being interesting. If you don't feel good about yourself, you are probably not very much fun to be around. The most important part of any relationship is how it makes you feel. When you take your eye off the relationship, you forget about the magic! Relationships thrive on attention and surprise. No one likes doing the same things every day because they are expected, and when things become so routine, it is easy to get bored and look for new stimulation elsewhere.

Each of us is on our own individual path, and where our paths collide, we unite. That doesn't automatically mean that you continue to be on the same path forever. We are individuals with individual needs and sometimes those needs change. It isn't anyone's fault; it just is the way it is. To deny that you have grown in another direction from someone you love does not feel true to yourself. You cannot live your life through someone else. It is often in not wanting to disappoint or hurt someone else that you get hurt. When you don't feel good, it doesn't benefit the relationship and it doesn't benefit you.

There are so many reasons for people staying together when, in their hearts, they know it is not the right thing to do. You have family and societal pressures, and it is often difficult to admit that you make mistakes. Sometimes you marry as a means of escape from living at home with your family, or as a means towards having children, and you feel the responsibility of your commitment weighing you down. You may be religious and feel that it is not morally right to divorce and carry that burden with you all your life. All of these situations do not make for a pleasant life. By suppressing your inner happiness, you are able to neither experience nor spread joy.

Staying together for your children, as admirable a goal as that may be, certainly doesn't feel good and more often than not leads to tension in the household, which is a far more injurious example to set for your children than by living lovingly apart. As long as children see love, they will be able to adapt to any situation. By always keeping in mind the reasons that you loved each other to start with, you can always find common ground to keep an open dialogue, even after the marriage has ended, and especially when children are involved.

To remember the past with love, make a list of the following things:

Think of the 20 funniest moments you shared together. If things ever get tense between you, rather than lose your temper, share one of the funny moments to immediately reduce the tension. If you can't think of 20 funny moments, it's probably a good thing you are no longer together.

Think about 10 positive things that you learned as a result of knowing your partner. Showing gratitude is the easiest and quickest way to release bitterness from your heart. When you look at the positive contribution to your life that each person brings for the duration of time they are in your life, you will live without regret.

List 10 positive things you would never have done if you were not with your partner. Each partner brings his or her individual desires into a relationship and by wanting to fulfil each other's desires you are able to experience new and exciting things. You may explore parts of the world you never thought about before, take up a new activity, move to a different location or meet a whole new group of people that have broadened your perspective forever.

If you have children, think of 20 of your partner's traits you would like them to have. When you are bitter about ending a relationship, sometimes you look at traits in your partner that are reflected in your children and can easily get into the habit of misplacing your frustrations. In any experience, when you look at the best things something has to offer, that is what you see. To keep on the high ground, look at the wonderful parts of each of you that your children share.

The quickest way to feel better at the end of a relationship is to get out there and try new things. Spread your wings a bit and see how much you have grown since you were last on your own. You have just figured out something important in your life about what you like and what you don't like. To change the future, put that knowledge into action.

- Move to a new location.
- See friends who have been neglected as a result of your relationship.
- Get into a new fitness regime.
- Take a class in something you have always wanted to learn.
- Change your appearance.
- Pamper yourself with time to relax and take it all in.

Coping with illness

I believe, and most health-care professionals would agree, that the attitude of the patient affects the overall benefits of whatever treatment plan is advised. This can conclusively be proven by the 'placebo effect', where a control group in scientific studies to test the effects of drug therapy are given nothing more than 'sugar pills'. In some cases, such as with anti-depressants, up to fifty per cent of those given the placebo improved anyway. It can certainly be argued that a percentage of them would have improved anyway, but similar percentages in most control groups, for many different drugs, also show improvement when they believe that the treatment can cure them.

Your expectations of illness often dictate how you feel, regardless of the real physical symptoms. Pain is often as a result of the *anticipation* of pain, rather than the real thing. An experiment in the use of ultra-sound to eliminate pain after a wisdom tooth extraction proved just as effective when the patient thought the machine was on, as when it was actually on. Sometimes, we react to what we think will be the end result rather than to the reality of the situation.

It is understandable how easy it is to focus on something that doesn't feel good because when things affect you physically, they are hard to ignore. If you break your predominant arm, you probably feel pain, and you also feel the frustration of not being able to do something that you are used to. You can use it as an excuse not to carry on with your normal activities, or you can look for other ways to do what you normally do – such as writing with or gaining strength in your other hand. It is by shifting the focus from what you can't do to a positive plan, that you will lessen the pain and improve your chances for wellness.

When you are ill, you have to want to feel better, as we discussed in looking at how to develop a positive mental attitude. The moment you begin to look at the limitations that an illness places on you, you are more likely to live up to those expectations. No matter what your life expectancy may be as a result of your illness, how you feel and what you are able to do will be, in large part, due to your attitude.

I have talked about the many miracles I have witnessed as a result of practising Reiki, and just yesterday I was surprised to get a knock on the door at 7 in the morning with the delivery of a case of wine. It was from a Reiki student who studied four levels of Reiki with me several years back and is a nurse in the healthcare system. The note just said, 'Thank you for the gift of Reiki.' It is one of the greatest miracles in my life. I was very moved and called to thank her, and she told me that her group had one of the highest success rates in her district – one patient was diagnosed with 5 weeks to live and is in great health two years on. She was overjoyed at being able to share her great faith in being able to improve upon people's physical condition by giving them hope for the future, as well as using all her medical and Reiki knowledge to help effect a cure.

There are many ways that you can choose to feel better when you are ill, if only for the moment. Anything that you can do to take your mind off the pain or the situation will make you feel better. Music is a great way to lift your spirits or transport you to another place, as is watching something that is funny or uplifting.

Ask some friends or loved ones to keep you company or engage in a project that keeps your mind occupied. Even when my best friend was weeks away from dying and in a hospice, she still had a desire to be creative and was determined to make a pot during a pottery class – one of the activities that the hospice provided. She did it and it gave her a sense of accomplishment that I am sure extended her life.

You can use many of the techniques in the previous chapters to put yourself in a better frame of mind. I can tell you, honestly, they really do work. Try anything and everything that you believe can make a difference to how you feel. When you are ill, it is a great to time to look at the important things in your life and make sure they are in order. It is the best time and gives a great sense of relief to finally let go of the insignificant things that really don't matter at all.

- Always take the advice of your medical carers, but if you have any doubts, seek another opinion.
- If you find that you have to wait in order to be treated, worrying about the outcome is the worst possible thing you can do. Try some complementary

therapies during the waiting time and do everything in your power to concentrate on feeling good.

- Sometimes life provides a contrast in order for you to appreciate what you have. Experiencing any type of illness can help you to pinpoint some areas in your life that require attention. Look at ways that you can improve your lifestyle to reduce the risk of illness.

Time marches on

With the ageing process come many life changes. The most apparent are the physical signs of ageing that may even begin to appear quite early in your life with the signs of your first grey hairs. If you are a woman, you will come to the change in your life where you are no longer able to have children, and with that may come physical symptoms associated with the menopause. If you have wanted children and been unable to have them, it can be a time in your life where you feel that there is no more hope. If you have had children and they leave home, it can be difficult to fill the void that your children have played in your happiness and the fulfilment in your life.

The same is true of a job or anything that you feel is lost as a result of getting older. If you hold on to the baggage of all that you think you have lost, it will be impossible to appreciate all the positive benefits that come with age. When you reach the time of your life when there are lesser pressures facing you on a daily basis, you can begin to spend more time fulfilling any of your personal desires that might have taken the back burner. There is nothing better to reverse the ageing process than to have some good old-fashioned fun, and I guarantee you, you can do that at any age.

There are two famous quotations from Satchel Paige, one

of the first black Americans to play baseball in the Major League. He continued to pitch in the major leagues until he was 59 years old, and during his last game, he pitched three shutout innings – meaning no runs were scored! When asked about his age, he never answered directly, and here are two of his best!

'How old would you be if you didn't know how old you are?'

'Age is a question of mind over matter – if you don't mind, it doesn't matter.'

I sincerely believe that age is a state of mind and have truly witnessed this throughout my life. Don't let the mental clutter get in the way of having the most fun in your lifetime.

Change your physical appearance

You have a great deal of control over how you look and feel, regardless of your age. If your appearance gets in the way of who you really feel like, do something about it. Don't let anyone pass judgement about how you feel about yourself. There are so many immediate ways to make yourself feel and look younger that are not drastic, that can take years off your age with little effort. It is often the fear of disapproval from others that limits your choices.

Although I have never gone in for cosmetic enhancements, I have absolutely no problem with those who feel that it will make a difference to their lives. Whatever works and feels best for you is the right thing to do. I have lots of friends who have had nips and tucks here and there, who feel far more optimistic about life. As long as how you look does not occupy an inordinate amount of your thoughts, you are on the right track for you.

Do what you have always wanted to do

It is natural, as you reach key birthdays in your life, to think about all that you have done or all that you want to do. In your younger years you are brimming with desires, wanting to experience lots of new things to see what feels the best. You are young enough to remember the fun you had playing around when you had less responsibilities, and probably made a great effort to incorporate fun things into your life.

As you get older and have more responsibilities, the demands that you place on yourself to be successful may overshadow your joyous spirit. All work and no fun make Jack and Jill very dull indeed. If you spend your life working towards some end and forget to maximize the enjoyment along the way, when you get to that end, you may find it quite disappointing. It is not the end but the journey that really matters. Many people become cynical as a result of getting to the end of their career and feeling that they have not accomplished what they set out to do. If you wait to have fun until you reach a certain stage in your life, you will always feel disappointed!

It's never too late to go after something you want, or to realize that something you always thought you wanted really isn't that important. Never let your physical age limit your desires! It is very easy to fall into the trap of 'acting your age' or believing that getting older must bring with it limitations. It really is true that you are only as old as you feel. You can feel young at heart whether you are 9 or 90, as long as you remember to have fun every day. Once you forget about your inner desire for playfulness and surprises, you can act older than your years.

Given the benefit of your years, what are the most important things to you now? Think about 10 ways that you can have more fun doing the things that you are currently doing; then think about the things you always wanted to do as soon as you had the time. There is no time like the present.

Refresh your home

The best way to signal a change in your lifestyle is to do something to mark the event. When your children leave home, it's a good time to re-assess your living arrangements. As your priorities change, you may find that you can use the additional space for things you want to do. You may also consider changing homes or moving to a different climate. As your children are beginning their own lives, it's a great time to begin the next cycle of your own life. Keeping in touch with your current desires keeps you in the present moment, rather than going back in time. What you were looking for in a home all those years ago may not be what you would choose today. Change is good and exciting and stretches you to new heights.

If you choose to adapt your current home to better fit your current circumstances, there are many ways of retaining dual functionality in your rooms for when your children come back home to visit. I have encountered so many people who leave things just as they were, to help them remember the experience of their children growing up, and also as a signal that it is always ok to come back home. Things don't have to be frozen in time to feel welcoming!

Accepting the unacceptable

Accepting death is never easy, no matter how far removed from the circumstances you may be. There is no rhyme or reason as to why and when we die and trying to figure out such matters can occupy your thoughts with no way of ever coming up with an answer. Rather than looking at why we die, the better approach is to look at why we live.

Each day you read the newspapers or watch the evening news and see the many tragedies that happen in your local community, your country and in the world. You will never figure out why these tragedies happen, but when they do happen, the lives that are lost never go unnoticed. As a result of atrocities, people and governments mobilize and do something to try to aid the situation. Look at all the wonderful efforts in the past century that have been made to wipe out hunger, poverty and senseless deaths. You can choose to look at the end result, rather than the cause.

The same is true when you face the personal loss of someone that you love. Rather than looking at the void that is created in your life as a result of the loss, by focusing on all the things that your loved one brought to your life experience, you can treasure the wonderful moments forever and know that your loved one was meant to be in your life for the purpose of bringing you joy that will last forever.

With loss often comes guilt; somehow believing that you could have done something differently to change the circumstances. I didn't feel great about having an argument with my father before he died and never getting to say I was sorry to him; however, I never did believe it was the cause of his death. I believe that your loved ones are always with you and I always have a mental chat with all of my friends and family who are no longer living and feel their presence with me often. It's never too late to say that you love them and hold them in your heart forever. I also believe, for the sake of their soul, you must let them move on by moving on in your own life.

If you are having a difficult time coming to terms with a personal loss, you may also experience feelings of restlessness, sleeplessness, agitation and depression. It is helpful to know that these are common reactions to the grieving process in order to not feel alone. Ask your family doctor to recommend therapists who may help. You may want to try some of the following complementary therapies to help you through the process:

If you have experienced the loss of a partner, you will miss the sense of personal contact. Aromatherapy or any form of massage can help you release some of the tensions and emotions and allow you to feel physical contact in a therapeutic setting.

Reiki is a wonderful therapy that can enable you to release emotional and mental blockages as a result of holding on to grief. A typical Reiki treatment is about an hour long and does not involve having to disrobe. Although traditionally practised by lightly placing the hands on energy centres throughout your body, it can be equally as effective without any bodily contact, so state your preference to the practitioner.

Any energy healing work will help.

The following exercise invokes your spiritual nature and may allow you to gain some peace and express your feelings to the loved one who has passed away. It can be a powerful exercise where you can feel a strong connection with the one you have lost and may even feel a spiritual connection by experiencing warmth in your hands or a feeling of a gentle breeze passing by. Let your emotions flow and do not be worried by any reactions you may have.

Begin by sitting in your most comfortable chair, and do the gentle breathing exercises (see page 73) until you feel yourself in a calm place. Imagine in your mind's eye a very happy occasion that you spent with your loved one and picture it in as much detail as possible. Do not worry if you cannot see it clearly – you may see it through a mist or fog or not really be able to picture it, but rather feel the experience. You are experiencing a very happy time and feel the connection that you have in this moment of joy. Now imagine that your loved one is with you this moment, right in front of you. Let them reassure you that they are well and listen to what advice they would give you about their dreams for your future. Imagine you can tell them everything that is in your heart and release all of your feelings of sadness by being aware that you will always know they are with you forever. As you begin to feel a sensation of well-being, imagine being bathed in a beautiful silver light that spreads love and light throughout the universe. Know that you can always come back to this time for a few minutes to feel the connection. Begin to slowly bring your awareness back to the present moment and gently wriggle your toes and fingers. In your own time, open your eyes and feel lighter and more appreciative of your connection with all that is.

9.

Ten Simple Strategies to Improve Your Day

Sometimes it is easy to think that life has to be complicated in order for you to get what you want, and that you have to suffer in the process. There is nothing in the rulebook that says it has to be hard. On the whole, we all want the same thing – to live a long and happy life. The best way to do that is to take simple steps each day towards that end.

You know what it takes to live a long life – look after your physical body and stay active mentally. There is nothing complicated in that, and it is well within your abilities to find many easy and fun ways of doing it throughout your lifetime.

Without even thinking, you could make a list of 20 possible ways for you to eat well and do more exercise and that wouldn't even stretch your imagination. If you didn't limit the possibilities in your mind, you could think of 100 fun ways to incorporate those things into your life. What you have to remember is, it doesn't take much effort to do those things, and all it takes is to remember the ultimate purpose in everything you do – a long and happy life. Then it's up to you to make these choices each day.

The only way to keep fit mentally is to continue to challenge your mind. Never ever rule out the possibility that you can learn new things. To stay mentally active, you have to have new stimulation daily to keep your mind occupied. You can read the paper to enable you to think and formulate your opinions – and maybe do a crossword; you can go to the movies and try to figure out what is going to happen at the end; or maybe you can just think about what you want to do at the end of the day or next week. Anything that keeps your mind active is a great fitness routine for the brain.

Happiness is really easy if you just look at all of the small things that can make you happy. If I asked you for 50 things that make you happy, I'm sure that you could come up with a list in very little time and would find that most of the things on the list you already have and are free. Why not look at all of the little things that you have close to hand that can put you in a happy frame of mind every day, and when you think about it, you will have achieved half of your lifelong goal.

No matter how you feel about your life in this moment, these simple strategies are guaranteed to make you feel better. They are easy to do, don't take up very much time, don't cost any money and they really do work. Once you begin to focus on your two main goals – long life and happiness – everything else will rapidly fall into place.

You can try one a day for the next ten days and look at the impact it has on your day, or try them all at the same time and feel the difference more quickly.

1. Smile

How many times do you think that you smile in the course of the day? Sure, you probably smile if you see something that makes you smile. But why wait for the universe to give you something to smile about? Take the initiative with a smile of your own and see how contagious it is. All you have to do is smile for as little as a few minutes to make a difference to how you feel and how people around you react.

I have a dear friend who told me a story from her childhood that illustrates this point. After school she was allowed to have an ice cream cone from the local shop. She would always stand in line and think about how delicious the ice cream would taste and just thinking about it would make her smile. When it was finally her turn, the vendor would always notice her great big smile and give her an extra large portion, so she learned to always smile at the ice cream man.

To see how a smile makes you feel, think back to your feelings when you had your first big crush on someone. You can probably still remember how you felt the first time they smiled at you. If you have children, you can probably remember the first thing that made them smile. Smiles are memorable because they warm our hearts. A smile is an outward reflection of what is in your heart that delights at the wonders and beauty of all that is around you. It is a universally recognized sign that means one thing, and one thing only – happiness and contentment in the moment.

Such a simple thing not only makes you feel good, it also makes everyone that you come in contact with feel good as well. Smiling is a win–win proposition and it gets you further towards achieving whatever you want while feeling good in the process. When you smile, you make a conscious effort to see things that please you. The funny thing is that you can always find something to smile about, even in difficult situations. All you have to do is think about something positive that has happened to you that makes you smile.

I bet you never thought that you could hear a smile, but you know what: you really can. A smile is so powerful that it can be transmitted down a phone line, in a letter, and across a crowded room. You can sense a smile on every level – even physically. Smiling and laughing are great for releasing endorphins, or happy hormones, into your brain, helping you to feel an overall sense of well-being.

Starting today, make a conscious effort to smile in the following situations:

- First thing in the morning
- When you look at yourself in the mirror
- When you see your partner/family members
- When you catch someone's eye
- When you sit down to eat a meal
- Whenever you go into a shop
- When you get to the office
- When you are on the phone
- When you write a letter
- When you do something you don't want to do
- When you are proud of something you've done.

Seeing is believing, so pay special attention to what happens as a result of taking the time to smile. See if you get extra ice cream, or a few extra flowers, or faster service, or feel happier to be alive. Isn't it always better to look for the things that please you rather than the minor annoyances that don't help you achieve the happiness you want and deserve?

2. Give yourself time in the morning to look your best

How you face the morning can impact on your feelings for the rest of the day. If you are the sort of person who stays in bed until the last minute, before throwing yourself together and out the door, your mind and body can spend the rest of the day trying to play catch-up. You never feel 'put-together' which makes it difficult to concentrate on what you hope to achieve. When you take the time to enjoy your personal grooming routines, collect your thoughts and have some breakfast, you are better able to focus on your desires for the day.

If you find you are tired and have a difficult time getting out of bed in the morning, perhaps your body requires more sleep. It is good to try to alter your sleep patterns by going to bed a bit earlier and getting up earlier in the morning. There is nothing like a peaceful house with no phones ringing or other people about to be able to appreciate the day. A good hot shower and scrub can invigorate you and get your brain cells grooving, especially if you use products with essential oils such as grapefruit, neroli and lavender. Not only will you feel good in the moment, but also the effects of the essential oil's fragrance can refresh you throughout the day.

Your drinking and eating habits will also impact on the amount of energy you have in the morning. If you find that you require too much sleep, you may be deficient in vitamins or require nutritional advice. Without the proper diet, your metabolism, which controls the processing of food and waste, can make you feel sluggish. There may also be medical reasons for low energy, so if it is persistent, you should visit your doctor.

To feel in control in the morning, try these helpful tips:

- Decide what you want to wear the night before and make sure your clothes are clean and in good order.
- Allow yourself an hour to get ready each morning.
- Always have a good look in the mirror and acknowledge what you see. Do your eyes sparkle? Is

your complexion in good shape? Do you look tired?
Take steps to improve conditions and don't forget to
look at all of the great things about you as well.

● Accentuate the positive.

● Spend at least 15 minutes sitting down to have some
breakfast. Eating on the run does not help your
digestion and doesn't allow you to appreciate your
food. Just think about how good it is to have
your morning coffee or tea and sip it casually,
rather than gulping it down on the run.

3. Start each day with a blank canvas

The more you are able to begin each day in the most positive
frame of mind, the better your chances of having a fantastic
day. This means taking each day as it comes, leaving behind
anything unpleasant or unresolved from the day before. It
gives you a fresh perspective and allows you to approach
things in a new and different way that will work to your
advantage in everything that you do. Being in an optimistic
frame of mind means that you see things working out for the
best. If you let past experiences dictate your future, you will
paint yourself into a box where each day you live old experiences again and again.

When you start your day looking backwards, it is hard to
play catch-up and you never feel like you can get ahead of
the game. Pretty soon, each day rolls into another day like a
continuing saga, rather than each day being nothing more
than a moment in time. Imagine a painting or a photograph
that captures a moment in time. If you take a picture in the
next moment, you may see something completely different.
Every moment is another opportunity to make the most of.

Hope is what keeps us going. If I asked you what you hoped for in the day, you would give me a positive answer. I hope to do this, or I hope to feel like that. I can't think of anyone who would hope for something bad to happen to them at any time. Yet, on a daily basis, you often set your expectations so very low by ruling out the possibility that things can be different today than they were yesterday.

Try this simple visualization before you get out of bed in the morning.

Imagine that you are leaving your house and you stop at the front door for a minute to check out the weather for the day. Is it one of the first beautiful mornings of springtime, when the sky is the most beautiful shade of blue with high fluffy clouds and the sun is shining brightly in the sky? As you set off on your day, you take a deep breath in to smell the newness of the season in the air. The leaves are beginning to bud on the trees and for the first time, you can feel the warmth in the sunshine. You look around you and begin to notice that everything is bursting into new growth. It seems like just yesterday it was cold and grey and everything looked dirty and dingy, and all of a sudden, it's like the curtains have been opened and everything looks fresh and new. You start thinking about all the things that you want to do in the day, and about how much nicer it is doing them when you feel renewed and invigorated.

As it's such a lovely morning, you decide you are going to walk a bit further than you usually do. On the way you are going to think of one thing that you would really like to do in the day. Whatever it is, imagine doing it. See yourself as clearly as you can, enjoying the moment. As you experience the pleasure of having what you want in the moment, know that you can have what you want in every moment – to feel the joy and excitement of the experience. All you have to do is want it. As you savour this moment, begin to bring your awareness back to your physical body. Shake out your legs and arms, take a few breaths and get ready to face this beautiful day.

Try this experiment to change your attitude about an expectation:

The next time you anticipate that something isn't going to work out, imagine that you can change the situation just by making up a different ending to the story. Think about the best possible result from the situation, and the next time you face the experience, go into it thinking that it is going to work out for the best. You will be very surprised to see how often it works – even for things that you seemingly have no control over.

For example:

If you hate waiting for public transportation, next time you go to catch the bus or train, imagine that it is there, waiting for you. You don't have to rush or worry that it won't be there, just see it arriving at just the right time for you. You will feel much better about the whole process, and I do believe you will find that it will work for you more often than not.

4. **Do something fun daily**

Remember the days when you were a child and you lived to have fun? You had fun on your way to school, you got to go outside and play during the day, and when you finished your homework at the end of the day, you were probably allowed to play then as well. You might have hung out with your friends, played games, gone out on adventures, played sports, or just shared the events of the day with your best mate. That was the time of day that you looked forward to most, and thinking about it helped to provide an incentive to get all of your work done. Having fun was something that you expected to do each and every day.

Do you still have the same expectations? Do you expect to get up every day and have some fun, or do you, like most, believe that you have to be serious to accomplish your goals? Having fun makes you feel light-hearted and joyous. It removes your mind from worrying thoughts and gives you an enormous amount of renewed energy – after all, don't forget your ultimate goal in life is to be healthy and happy. What better way to get you there? In every respect, having fun makes you feel good physically, mentally and emotionally.

The funny thing is, all it takes to have fun in everything that you do, is to allow yourself the experience. It is good to have fun. It makes everything that you do easier and more pleasurable. It makes you be the type of person everyone wants to be around. When you think about the people in your life who you would like to spend more time with, aren't they the ones you have the most fun with? Why limit the amount of fun that you have to the occasional weekend or a couple of weeks a year? Surely, it is far better for you and for those around you when you spread out the fun across all 365 days of the year.

Look at some of the ways you can bring your playful nature into all of your daily activities:

- Wear something fun to work – experiment with colours or accessories to keep you in a cheerful frame of mind.
- Play a game on the way to work rather than worrying about traffic or public transportation. I Spy worked when you were a kid, so why not try it when you are a grown-up.
- Share a joke with someone in the course of your day. It puts you and the recipient in a good mood for the next segment of their day.
- Do something fun during your lunch break. Meet a friend for lunch, go for a picnic on the grass in the nearest green space, go to an exhibition, or go shopping. Having fun in the middle of your day makes the rest of the day go more quickly.
- Add some fun to your household chores. Turn on your favourite music and sing and dance to your heart's content while you prepare the food, do the vacuuming, or anything else that isn't normally fun. By adding fun to the process, you don't even notice that it was something you didn't look forward to doing.
- Plan at least one fun thing to do with your partner/ family each day. If you don't schedule the time, it is easy to get out of the routine of sharing pleasurable moments together.

5. **Make music**

One of the quickest ways immediately to change how you feel is to incorporate some music into your life on a daily basis. Sound creates vibrations that can alter your personal vibration and help you to immediately feel better. The ability to appreciate and respond to music is usually with you for the duration of your lifetime and is unaffected by most illnesses or injuries. Music therapy is used to help alleviate depression, lessen pain, and can be beneficial as a way of keeping your mind stimulated as you get older.

From the time you were a child, singing and music have had a huge impact on your life. When you were a baby, your parents probably sang you a lullaby to get you to go to sleep. You might have learned things like your ABC to music, and as you reached adolescence, choosing the type of music that you liked was probably one of the first defining moments between your choices and those of your parents. Music is something that you can appreciate on your own and an easy way for you to choose the way you want to feel in any moment.

Music also helps you to express feelings that you may not be able to verbalize. Singing a meaningful song out loud can help say something to someone without having to put yourself on the line. We all have songs that we use to express our emotions and may sing them as a sign of what is happening emotionally inside.

If you are really tense, listening to soothing music can help to relieve the tension by releasing your nervous energy. Conversely, if you are lacking in energy, some good old rock and roll can shake you into a sense of well-being.

The more you actively participate by singing, whistling, or humming, the more quickly you will feel the positive influences in your physical body as well as your mind. Why not start your day by singing in the shower and see how good it makes you feel.

Start by making a list of your favourite songs to:

- Get you moving
- Help you relax
- Get you in a romantic mood
- Sing along to.

Always have some of your favourites close to hand when you need them. With the wonder of technology, you can download a CD of your favourites in a matter of minutes. Why not get a feel-good collection together for different needs and see how they instantly improve how you feel.

6. Do something different

There's nothing better to get some excitement back into your life than to venture outside your comfort zone. It is so easy to fall into routines of doing the same things day in and day out. You eat the same foods, go to the same places, see the same friends, buy the same clothes, do the same job, and pretty soon your life becomes so predictable that you no longer have any expectations. Wake up! There is a whole world out there waiting to be experienced.

To change your outlook for the future, you need to continuously try new things. What do you have to lose? The worst thing that can happen is that you don't like the experience, and you don't have to do it again. If you don't keep yourself stimulated, you become a very boring person.

- Change your hairstyle
- Wear new colours
- Speak to a stranger
- Listen to a different type of music
- Venture to a new part of town
- Try an ethnic food that you have never eaten
- Say something you have always wanted to say
- Learn to swim/dance/play tennis
- Challenge your mind by taking a class
- Go for a hike in the woods
- Read different types of books
- Take up a new hobby
- Set a new record for a personal best
- Take off a day in the middle of the week just to relax and have fun.

7. Connect with nature

We all spend too much time thinking and not enough time experiencing what is going on around us. One of the easiest ways to feel more grounded, or connected to the earth, is to get outdoors and enjoy the natural wonders of the earth. The colours of nature are uplifting and there is a sense of optimism that can be gained by looking at the life cycles that occur as the seasons change. I bet, when you think about it, some of the most memorable times in your life occurred outdoors – playing on a beach, taking a walk in the woods, going for a swim or just having a picnic.

One of the most uplifting experiences I have is taking my dogs for a walk in the park early in the morning. Whether it is in the dead of winter or in the middle of summer, early morning is the most peaceful time of the day. The dew is still on the ground, the silence of the morning allows you to hear the birds singing, and people who are up at that time of the morning smile as they pass you by. It is the easiest way for you to clear the cobwebs from your mind and get ready to face the day.

For an instant pick me up any time of the day, try the following:

Get up an hour earlier and go for a morning walk or run. Head for the nearest green space and take in all the details of the experience. Smell the flowers and the earthy scent of the soil. Listen to the sounds of the birds or water. Look at the amazing colours in the leaves, flowers and sky. Touch the bark of a tree or the smoothness of a leaf. Feel your connection to the earth as you walk purposefully. Not only will it make you feel great mentally, it is a fantastic way of getting physical exercise into your routine at the start of the day.

Have your lunch outdoors when you can. Bring a book and your favourite packed lunch and find a nice place to sit where you can soak up the elements. The sun is essential in producing Vitamin D that keeps your bones strong and your skin clear. It is recommended that we all have 30 minutes of sunshine a day. Allow 10 minutes of sunshine before putting on sun cream to allow the Vitamin D production.

Do some gardening. Whether you have green space as part of your home, or just a few potted plants in your house, getting your hands in the soil is the best way to relieve excess nervous energy. All you have to do is imagine that as you place your hands in the earth, your excess energy goes into the earth to be grounded. You can believe it, or not, but it instantly works.

Walk around barefoot. A great way to gain physical energy from the earth is to walk barefoot in the grass. If you are lacking in energy, sit in a chair or bench outdoors with your bare feet on the earth. Close your eyes and imagine that the low-vibration earth energy is able to connect through the bottom of your feet and rise up to your knees. You may feel a sensation of tingling as this happens. You will feel physically more energized and it only takes a few minutes.

Plan a family meal outdoors when the weather is fine. Everyone will remember the occasion as it is not something you do daily. It is a great way to wind down after a day's work, or a special treat to look forward to on a weekend.

8. Look at something beautiful

One of the quickest ways to get your heart in gear is to look at something that is beautiful to you. It can be as simple as waking up and looking around at your loved ones, or even things in your home that bring you pleasure, like a beautiful plant or a lovely picture.

Sometimes it is easy to get tears of joy, simply by appreciating the beauty in a person, place or thing. Think about the feeling you get when you look at a baby, bend down to pat a puppy, or watch someone perform an amazing feat, like winning an Olympic gold medal. Even if these experiences are not directly related to you, you feel a sense of joy, just for the pleasure of seeing something that delights you.

When you choose to look at the beauty around you on a daily basis, it puts you in a positive frame of mind and helps to relieve troubling thoughts. The more small, positive steps that you take during the day to feel good, the happier and more productive you will be.

Try this little experiment for one day to see how it feels when you deliberately choose to look at the beauty around you. All it takes is a few seconds to feel the pleasure that beauty of all types can bring to your life.

- Look for the five most beautiful things in your home.
- What is the most beautiful thing about the area you live in?
- Look for the most beautiful colour that you see during your day.
- Look for the best-dressed man that you see.
- Look for the best-dressed woman that you see.
- Look for the most beautiful clothes that you see in a shop window.
- Look for the most beautiful face that you see where you work.
- Look for the most beautiful thing that you see in nature.

9. Plan time to relax

Just as it is important to start your day with enough time to get geared up for your daily activities, it is equally important to allow your body to unwind in order to release the minor tensions and stresses that can easily accumulate in a hectic day. It is really good to have at least 30 minutes of personal time just to yourself.

When you are in a relaxed frame of mind you are far happier to deal with the small things that you may have to do at the end of the day for yourself or your family.

To help you immediately wind down, get out of your work kit as soon as you get home. Pick comfortable clothing that isn't restricting, that enables you to feel relaxed.

Water is a great element of purification. Something as simple as washing your face when you get home at the end of the day can help you to wash away the worries and cares of the day. If you have had a physically exhausting day, there's nothing like a hot soak in the tub with essential oils to instantly get rid of the tension.

Reading a book is a great means of escape and allows your brain a good workout in the process. Using your imagination to transport you to another place in time stimulates all of your creative senses. Newspapers can be depressing, so stick to something that you find relaxing to help you wind down.

Watching something funny or uplifting on television is also a great way to take your mind off the events of the day. Make sure it is something that you really want to watch to get the most benefit from the experience. It is very easy to get into the habit of mindlessly watching the tube and not interacting with those around you.

Indulge yourself in a glass of wine, a cocktail or a lovely cup of tea – whatever helps you to relax the most. Find your favourite spot in the house or garden and put your feet up and do nothing!

10. Show appreciation

Doesn't it feel fantastic to be appreciated? Think about the last time someone thanked you for something. You don't have to do something grand to make a difference. Just knowing that even a small action of yours had an impact on something or someone puts a smile on your face and causes a stirring in your heart. We all like to know that our actions are worthwhile. It is a way of knowing that you are on track and seeing the important things that happen around you every day.

There are many ways to show appreciation, but it all starts with appreciating yourself and everything that you have in your life. It doesn't take very long to feel the difference – just a few minutes at the start and end of your day.

To begin the day, be thankful for everything you have.

> Take a few minutes, before you rush out of bed, to get centred. Take a deep breath in to the count of five and exhale to the count of five and do this several more times until you feel nice and relaxed. Bring your awareness to your surroundings and take in all the things that you have as a result of all of your efforts. Think of the home that you live in, the lovely furniture or pictures, all of your clothing and other possessions, and really look at what you have. Think about all of the people that have helped you to get where you are and, from your heart, send a special thank you. When you are finished, thank the universe out loud for all that you have. Slowly begin to wriggle your toes and shake out your arms and feel grateful that your body serves you well.

During the day, try the following:

Everything or everybody that you appreciate provides pleasure in your life. Think about sitting down to eat the most sumptuous meal you have ever had and I bet you can remember everything about the experience. Your appreciation of the food made the experience a delight. Think about the last time you praised someone for a job well done. I bet the next job they did was even better. Showing appreciation allows the things you love to grow.

Take the time to appreciate your food. When you see how lovely it looks and smells and take the time to be aware of the taste, it forces you to eat more slowly, which has the added benefit of aiding your digestion. You will also feel more satisfied with the quantity by relishing each mouthful.

Always show appreciation to the many nameless people that make your life run more smoothly. The postmen, rubbish collectors and street cleaners who you see each day and probably never speak to, deserve your gratitude for making your life more pleasant.

Say thank you to all the shop assistants or waiters/waitresses who serve you each day. It helps them to know that what they do counts in making the day just a bit better for you.

Tell the people you work with how important they are in helping you to accomplish your goals. It is a great way to ensure that you always get help when you need it.

Accept compliments graciously. When someone says well done, allow yourself to fully feel the meaning of the words. It will help to build your self-confidence and

it will enable you to see how good it feels to be
appreciated.

Look after your material possessions and appreciate
how much time and energy it took you to get them.
Hang up your clothes, look after your shoes and
appreciate your home by taking care of it each day.

Tell your loved ones each day how much you
appreciate them being a part of your life. A little goes a
long, long way!

Conclusion: The Power of Intention

Throughout this book I hope that I have been able to show you ways to use your amazingly powerful mind to look at all that life has to offer, rather than at the disappointments you may have faced in the past. Your desire, or intention, is all that you need to begin the process of living life to the fullest and experiencing the best each moment has to offer. All you have to do is look for it as much as you possibly can.

The best way to do this is to remember the childlike wonder of experiencing things for the first time. It is ever so easy to let life become boring and humdrum by doing the same old thing every day. Just by looking at everything with the intention of soaking it all up, absorbing all the colours, sights, smells, sounds, tastes, people and amazing energy available to you through so many sources, you can always bring yourself to a place of happiness, no matter how far away from that you may be in the moment. It just takes practice to keep remembering to get enthusiastic and excited about everything you do. It is more fun and even chores go by more quickly.

We all stray from the path of knowing what is right for us and that is part of our life experience. We get angry over silly things, stick to our principles, often out of stubbornness, eat too much, drink too much, spend too much and do things that, given the benefit of hindsight, we wish we hadn't. I'm sure my husband would be willing to share many of my imperfections, given the opportunity!

The trick is not to beat yourself up, but rather accept your humanity and try to do better next time. Say you are sorry to anyone you may have hurt in the process and let it go rather than allowing the emotional clutter to build up and clog your heart and mind. It is the only way to build your self-esteem. Being able to accept your weaknesses is the first step on the path to self-enlightenment. Once you are aware, you can do something about it. It is a way of starting a new cycle in your life that can be transformational.

Your life will still have moments that you would not choose to repeat, as without these experiences you could not continue to grow and define what is most important to you. By detaching yourself from things and experiences that do not help you to achieve what you want, you will always be receptive to new ideas. This is essential in helping you to de-junk your mind from the old way of doing things and look at all the ways that you can take positive steps forward to get what you want.

Your life may not dramatically change overnight, but I promise you that with an open mind and an open heart, where there is a will, there is a way. Try it and see how much better it is to choose to feel good.

Contacts

Complementary Therapies

Aromatherapy
International Federation of
Aromatherapists
Call for information on
how to locate local
practitioners.
020 8742 2605
http://www.int-fed-aroma
therapy.co.uk

Crystal Healing
Affiliation of Crystal
Healing Organizations
P.O. Box 100
Exminster
Exeter
01479 841450

Flower Remedies
Dr Edward Bach Centre
Mount Vernon
Sotwell
Wallingford
Oxfordshire
OX10 1PZ
01491 834678
http://www.bachcentre.com

Homeopathy
Society of Homeopaths
11 Brookfield
Duncan Close
Moulton Park
Northampton
NN3 6WL
0845 450 6611
http://
www.homeopathy-soh.com

Light Therapy
SAD Association (SADA)
PO Box 989
Steyning
East Sussex
BN44 3HG
01903 814942
http://www.sada.org.uk

Meditation
Transcendental Meditation
Call for details of your
nearest centre
0800 269303
http://www.t-m.org.uk

Reiki
Reiki Healers & Teachers
Society
020 8776 0546
http://www.reikihealersand
teachers.net

Stress Management
International Stress
Management Association
P.O. Box 348
Waltham Crescent
London
EN8 8ZL
07000 780430
http:://www.isma.org.uk

Yoga
The British Wheel of Yoga
25 Jermyn Street
Sleaford
Lincolnshire
NG34 7RU
01529 306851
http://www.bwy.org.uk

Helplines

Bereavement
Cruse Bereavement Line
National line: 0870 167
1677
http://www.caritas.
data.co.uk

Emotional Support
Samaritans
0845 790 9090
www.samaritans.co.uk

Daily Motivation
Thought for Today
www.innerspace.org.uk/
home/thoughtfortoday.asp

*Free Courses on Self
Development*
www.brahmakumaris.
org.uk

Acknowledgements

With appreciation:
My husband Jerry, who always has the right words at the right time and whose confidence in my abilities always helps me to achieve my goals.

My family in America and England who show such love and support.

Kate Adams and all the team at Penguin for their enthusiasm and input into the project.

Celia Worster for her spiritual insight and wonderful aromatherapy.

Delacy Kirby for sharing her wonderful healing experiences.

I am forever grateful for my wise and wonderfully talented network of friends whose insights and life experiences have contributed greatly to this book: Ann, Caroline, Cat, David, Gaby, Jane, Joannie, Judy, Karen, Kate, Londa, Matt, Nina, Phil, Rupert, Sally O', Sam, Sara, Sarina, Sergio, Susie, Tessa, Tibye, Victoire and VM2.

WIN A ONE-ON-ONE CONSULTATION WITH DAWNA WALTER!

wna Walter has turned her famous techniques de-cluttering to that most important area of all he mind.

d you could be the lucky recipient of a one-on-e consultation to have your mind de-junked!

wna Walter will spend a day helping you to k-start your de-junking process. During the visit, she will look at ur current habits and routines, discuss areas in your life that you uld like to improve, and develop a personal action plan to keep u focused on your goals. A 30-day follow-up consultation will be anged via correspondence or e-mail.

be in with a chance of winning this exclusive prize, simply send ostcard including your name, address, email and telephone mber to the following address: Dawna Walter Competition, nguin General Marketing, 80 Strand, London, WC2R 0RL.

sing date for entries is 31st July 2005.

ake the PLUNGE and CHANGE our life for the better ... NOW!